The Mannequins' Ball

Polish Theatre Archive
A series of books edited by Daniel Gerould, Graduate School, City University of New York, USA

This book is part of a series. The publisher will accept continuation orders which may be cancelled at any time and which provide for automatic billing and shipping of each title in the series upon publication. Please write for details.

The Mannequins' Ball

A play in three acts
by Bruno Jasieński

*translated and with
an introduction by*
Daniel Gerould

 **harwood academic publishers**
Australia • Canada • France • Germany • India
Japan • Luxembourg • Malaysia • The Netherlands
Russia • Singapore • Switzerland

Amsteldijk 166
1st Floor
1079 LH Amsterdam
The Netherlands

All inquiries concerning performance rights should be addressed to: Samuel French, 45 West 25th Street, New York, NY 10010, USA

British Library Cataloguing in Publication Data

Jasieński, Bruno, 1901–1939
    The mannequins' ball: a play in three acts. – (Polish and
    east European archive)
    1. Experimental drama, Polish – Translations into English
    I. Title   II. Gerould, Daniel, 1928–
    891.8'527

    ISBN 90-5755-052-0

Cover illustration: A woodcut by Dmitri Moor from the original 1931 Moscow edition.

CONTENTS

INTRODUCTION TO THE SERIES

The *Polish Theatre Archive* makes available in English translation major works of Poland's dramatic literature as well as monographs and critical studies on playwrights, theatre artists, theatres and stage history. Although emphasis is placed on the contemporary period, the *Polish Theatre Archive* also encompasses the nineteenth-century roots of modern theatre practice in Romanticism and Symbolism. The individual plays will contain authoritative introductions that place the works in their historical and theatrical contexts.

Daniel Gerould

Portrait of Bruno Jasieński by Tytus Czyżewski, 1920

LIST OF PLATES

The plates in the text reproduce the original woodcuts by Moor
from the 1931 Moscow edition of the play (David Goldfarb,
graphic reproduction)

Portrait of Bruno Jasieński by Stanisław Ignacy Witkiewicz, 1921

CHRONOLOGY OF THE LIFE AND WORK OF BRUNO JASIEŃSKI

1901   Born July 19, in Klimontów, a small town near Sandomierz (in
           the Russian sector of occupied Poland), where his father, Jakub
           Zysman, is a country doctor. Jakub changes the family name to
           Jasieński to conceal their Jewish origins.

1914–18   Spends the war years with his family in Moscow. Discovers
           Mayakovsky and the the Russian Futurists, while completing
           his secondary education at a Polish gymnasium.

1918   Returns to Poland and enrolls as a student in the philosophy
           department at Jagellonian University in Cracow.

1919   Establishes an amateur theatrical company in Klimontów,
           where he stages his own reworking of Wyspiański's *The
           Wedding*. With Anatol Stern, Aleksander Wat, Tytus Czyżewski,
           and Stanisław Młodożeniec founds Polish Futurism and
           organizes the Futurist club "Katarynka."

1921   Issues "Manifesto to the Polish People about the Immediate
           Futurization of Life" and "Manifesto about Futurist Poetry"
           and gives poetry readings with the Cracow and Warsaw
           Futurists including Stern and Wat. Publishes his first book of
           poetry, *A Boot in the Buttonhole*, in which he strikes the pose of
           a Futurist dandy.

1922   Publishes the long poem, *A Song of Hunger*, strongly influ-
           enced by Mayakovsky, which marks his commitment to engaged
           literature.

1923   Announces his closure on Futurism and refers to himself as a
           "former Futurist." Deeply affected by workers' uprising in
           Cracow. Publishes the grotesque tale, *The Legs of Izolda Morgan*.

An enthusiastic welcome for Jasieński in Moscow, May 22, 1929

1924   Moves to Lwów and becomes literary editor of the Communist newspaper, *The Workers' Tribune*. Works with a leftist theatre. Co-authors with Anatol Stern *Earth Leftward*, a collection of revolutionary poetry dedicated to "mass man," the hidden hero of history.

1925   Hampered by censorship and harassed by the police, leaves in the spring for France as a correspondent for a local Polish newspaper. In Paris works with the French Communist Party in the Polish émigré community.

1926   Publishes in Paris *The Lay of Jakub Szela*, about the Szela rebellion of 1848, combining avant-garde technique and folk poetry in a celebration of social revolution.

1927–28   Establishes an agit-prop theatre group in Paris, The Workers' Stage, for which he adapts *The Lay of Jakub Szela*.

     Denounced by the Polish Embassy and persecuted by the French police, the production is given at several workers' centers. Serves as a model for French Agit theatre.

1928   Writes the radical novel, *I Burn Paris*, as a response to Paul Morand's *Je brûle Moscou*, an anti-Soviet novel. It is published in installments in the French communist newspaper *L'Humanité*.

1929   *I Burn Paris* is published as a book by Flammarion; it also appears in the USSR and Poland.

     The French authorities order Jasieński deported to Germany. 40 French intellectuals including Barbusse and Rolland sign a petition asking the government to revoke its decision. Jasieński re-enters France illegally, is arrested and sent under escort to the German border. Unwelcome in Germany, takes a ship to the USSR.

     May 21, arrives in Leningrad, greeted by a large crowd including many reporters and writers. The next day arrives by train in Moscow. Adopts Russian citizenship.

     Paris is Burning, an adaptation of *I Burn Paris*, is played briefly in Russia in a production by the touring theatre Akvarium.

1929–30   Joins RAPP (Russian Association of Proletarian Writers); elected to the Secretariat of the Moscow section of RAPP; and becomes editor-in-chief of the newly established Polish-language magazine, *The Culture of the Masses*, whose aim is to involve the Polish minority living in the USSR in the creation of the new proletarian literature.

1930   Gives up the editorship of *The Culture of the Masses* (attacked for "nationalistic bolshevism") and devotes his energies to work in the International Section of RAPP called MORP (the International Association of Proletarian Writers) which at the time had seven sections: German, Hungarian, Austrian, Czech, American, Polish and Japanese. Serves as one of the organizers of the International Congress of Revolutionary Writers (held in Kharkov). Becomes editor-in-chief of the new periodical, *Literature of the World Revolution*, published in Russian, German, English, and French.

Sayoku Gekijyo, a left-wing theatre in Tokyo, plans to stage *Paris is Burning*, a Japanese adaptation of *I Burn Paris*, but the production is banned by the police.

1931   Publishes *The Mannequins' Ball* in Russian, with an introduction by Anatolii Lunacharsky. The play also appears in all foreign-language editions of *Literature of the World Revolution*.

1933   September 21, world premiere in Prague of *The Mannequins' Ball* at E. F. Burian's Theatre D34, with stage design by Antonin Heythum, Czech constructivist artist. The second production of the theatre, given only a limited number of performances because of threats of censorship.

In November Meyerhold declares his intention of staging *The Mannequins' Ball* (project never realized).

Witold Wandurski, playwright and director active in the Polish workers' theatre in the USSR, arrested.

1934   Publishes *Man Changes his Skin*, a socialist-realist novel about the construction of an irrigation canal in Soviet Tadzhikistan. Written in Russian and cast in the form of a detective story, the novel goes through nine editions in the next two years.

Wandurski executed.

1937   Starts the novel *The Conspiracy of the Indifferent*, which remains unfinished.

July 31, arrested on charges of deviation from the Party Line, nationalism, and treasonous contacts with enemies. Imprisoned in the Butyrki prison in Moscow for the next thirteen and a half months.

1938   September 17, found guilty, sentenced to death, and executed all on the same day in Moscow.

1955   Posthumously cleared of false charges and rehabilitated in the USSR.

1957   July 21, Polish premiere of *The Mannequins' Ball* in Katowice at the Teatr Śląski, directed by Jerzy Jarocki with stage design by Wiesław Lange.

1974   November 16, Warsaw premiere of *The Mannequins' Ball* at the Ateneum, directed by Janusz Warmiński with stage design by Krzysztof Pankiewicz.

1975   The Ateneum takes *The Mannequins' Ball* on tour to Hanover, Germany.

1976   Russian premiere of *The Mannequins' Ball* in Chelyabinsk, USSR, directed by Jerzy Jarocki.

1977   The Ateneum takes *The Mannequins' Ball* on tour to Moscow and Leningrad.

Collage design by Mieczysław Szczuka with portrait of Bruno Jasieński, 1924

Drawing by Antonin Heythum for the set of the world premiere at E.F. Burian's theatre collective D34. Prague, 21 September, 1933

INTRODUCTION

Jasieński, Lunacharsky, Moor, and *The Mannequins' Ball*

The Polish poet Bruno Jasieński was thirty-one when in 1931 he published his play *The Mannequins' Ball* in Moscow in Russian translation. Jasieński was then at the height of his power and prestige as an international Communist celebrity. He had arrived in the USSR two years earlier to much acclaim as a victim of political persecution in the capitalist West, having first been hounded by the Polish police and then deported from both France and Germany. At first a hero in the land of Lenin, Jasieński was made editor-in-chief of both the Polish-language *Culture of the Masses* and the new international *Literature of the World Revolution*, where *The Mannequins' Ball* appeared in the English, French, and German editions. He immediately became involved in the literary and cultural ideological wars that made the Soviet Union in the 1930s a very dangerous place, especially for true believers in Communism from abroad. Stalin ruthlessly eliminated these foreign Marxists who had sought refuge in what they imagined would be a socialist utopia.

Jasieński was by nature an *enfant terrible* who thrived on scandal and controversy. Arrogant and self-possessed, he had always known how to defend himself by going on the attack. His initial inspiration came from the Russian Cubo-Futurists and Mayakovsky. As an adolescent, he had spent the war years with his family in Moscow before returning to Poland in 1918.

A handsome brunet with a thin, nervous face, Jasieński began his career in Warsaw as a brash young Futurist poet with a fondness for elegant clothes. He wore a monocle in his right eye, knotted a bright red scarf around his neck, and carried a cane with a silver handle. The impression he created was studiedly theatrical.

In the early 1920s Jasieński traveled about Poland, reading his poetry and organizing evenings devoted to avant-garde art that often involved the participation of local actors. The poet's nonchalant manner – hands in pocket and monotone delivery – served as a deliberate provocation, drawing down the wrath of the public, the critics, and the local authorities. His conversion to Communism made Jasieński even less acceptable to the Polish state, already veering to the right. He moved to Paris, where he started a Polish workers' theatre. Booted out of France as a subversive alien, Jasieński eventually made his way to the USSR in 1929, bringing with him the text of his play about rebellious Parisian fashion mannequins.

In 1931 when his Introduction to *The Mannequins' Ball* was published with the play, Anatolii Lunacharsky was only fifty-eight but already seemed to be an old man. He had aged prematurely and was in poor health. Balding, with a short, straggly beard, sloping shoulders, pince-nez, and shapeless brown suits, the People's Commissar for Education looked more like a professor than a politician. Eased out of his position of authority in 1929, Lunacharsky was now a ghost of the past. As an old Bolshevik from the cultured intelligentsia, his influence was fading fast in the new age of Stalinism. In the early and mid-1920s as cultural commissar, Lunacharsky sought to retain the best of Western bourgeois culture, encouraged variety and experimentation in the theatre, and tolerantly worked for a balance between the old and new. By 1931 much of what he stood for in the arts was in the process of being swept away. Once Stalin had fully consolidated power, Lunacharsky became a figurehead, honorifically shunted aside with an appointment as Ambassador to Spain in 1932. He died in the south of France on the way to his assignment.

To understand why the former Commissar came to the defense of the former Futurist poet, we must look more closely at the polemics that dominated the cultural scene in the late 1920s and early 1930s. In the years 1928 to 1932 acrimonious controversy raged as to the future direction of Soviet art, literature, and theatre. The Russian Association of Proletarian Writers, known by its acronym RAPP, was an organization of fanatical communist writers mainly of non-proletarian origin who, in the name of ideological orthodoxy, fought among themselves and terrorized their literary adversaries, denouncing them as class enemies. Writers were increasingly obliged to conform to the strict party line. Both Mayakovsky and Jasieński joined RAPP. The RAPP theoreticians, aggressive younger writers and bureaucrats in quest of power, sought a monopoly in all cultural spheres, including theatre. Their technique was to vilify their enemies, who included other members of the organization.

The RAPP ideologues theorized endlessly, arguing that dialectical materialism was the sole basis of proletarian theatre and insisting that actors perform dialectically. They denounced the Soviet avant-garde of the early 1920s as bourgeois elitism, rejecting *a priori* the social satire and poster aesthetics of Meyerhold and Eisenstein. They attacked Mayakovsky mercilessly and were delighted with the failure of his *Bathhouse*, thus contributing to the pressures that drove the poet to his suicide on April 14, 1930. Finally, in 1932, fearing any ideological position other than abject submission to his will, Stalin abolished RAPP, along with all other literary organizations, and established a single Union of Soviet Writers in order to have total personal domination. At the first congress of the Writers' Union in 1934 socialist realism was declared to be the sole acceptable artistic method.

When Lunacharsky came to Jasieński's defense in 1931 and argued for the poet's freedom to write his play according to fantastic postulates and poster-like stylization, it was as though the former Commissar clearly saw the dangers that were threatening the Polish poet. In his introduction to *The Mannequins' Ball*, Lunacharsky refers specifically to the RAPP dogmas about the method of dialectical materialism (without ever naming the organization), and he allies himself with Jasieński as a proponent of imaginative freedom.

At first Jasieński himself did not realize the gravity of his situation. He had proved adept at outmaneuvering the Polish, French, and German police; the worst that they could do was to ban his books and expel him beyond their borders. The Polish poet soon discovered that, on the contrary, in the Soviet Union the problem for the nonconformist writer was the impossibility of ever getting out. Jasieński knew of the arrest in 1934 of Witold Wandurski, a Polish playwright and theatre worker, and of his execution the following year, as well as of the subsequent liquidation of almost all the leading Polish Communists living in the USSR.

In order to save himself, Jasieński tried everything – admission of errors, denunciation of others (including his wife), letters to Stalin, recantations, and confessions to crimes he had not committed. Nothing could save him. Conflicting reports have long circulated about the date and place of Jasieński's death, the most frequent being that he died of typhus on the way to a labor camp in Kolyma above the Arctic Circle in Siberia. Eyewitnesses reported seeing the emaciated poet in various Far Eastern prisons. Recently accessible documents show that Jasieński never left Moscow. He was arrested on July 31, 1937, imprisoned in Moscow, and tried, convicted, sentenced and shot on a single day, September 17, 1938. Jasieński's Mannequin-Leader, trapped in the world of capitalist intrigue, almost fell a victim to the duel he unwittingly provoked; at the last minute he leapt out the window. His creator had no such means of escape.

The eight woodcuts that accompanied both the Russian and the foreign-language editions of *The Mannequins' Ball* are by Dmitri Stakhievich

Orlov (1883–1946), a graphic artist and caricaturist who used the pseudonym Moor (after Karl Moor in Schiller's *The Robbers*). Moor was one of the principal creators of satirical political posters in the USSR and an important illustrator for Soviet books and magazines (including advertisements).

The son and grandson of Cossacks, Moor – a big, heavy-set, jovial man with intense light-blue eyes – sometimes wore the high-pointed hat and colorful costume of his ancestors, or he dressed carelessly in a simple belted blouse and peasant coat. Unconcerned with worldly trappings, he loved birds and animals and turned part of his apartment into an aviary where he kept hundreds of pigeons and a raven named Vanka to whom he talked.

Largely self-taught as an artist, Moor, who had wanted to be an opera singer, turned to political cartooning after taking part in the Revolution of 1905. He studied briefly at the studio of P. I. Kelin (1910), worked for the magazine *Budilnik (Alarm Clock)*, created the designs for the first agit-trains and a few ROSTA windows, and provided illustrations for *Izvestiya, Pravda, Krasnoarmeets,* and *Krokodil.* He was the art director of the anti-religious magazines *Bezbozhnik (The Atheist)* and *Bezbozhnik u Stanka (The Atheist at the Workbench)*, a member of the Group October, and a teacher at VKhUTEMAS/VKhUTEIN (Higher Artistic and Technical Studios/Institute) in Moscow, where he became a leading figure in the world of Soviet art education. He also designed the decorations for mass spectacles and political festivals and exhibited in Paris, Berlin, and Danzig (Gdańsk).

Moor's eight woodcuts tell the story of Jasieński's play in a visual idiom, revealing clearly the work's underlying emphasis on design and formal patterning. The intertwined themes of *The Mannequins' Ball* are fashion and dance. Craving the movement and freedom denied them in their servitude to humans, the headless tailors' mannequins stage their annual ball in the salon of a Parisian fashion house while the employees are out on strike. When the Leader of the socialist workers' party chances upon the mannequins' ball (as he lustfully pursues a female mannequin, thinking she is a woman), he is condemned by a court composed of tailors' dummies to have his head cut off by means of a giant pair of scissors struck with an iron. The mannequin who found the scissors claims the head, puts it on his shoulders, and dashes off to a human ball at the mansion of the tycoon and car manufacturer Arnaux. Regarded as the socialist labor leader by all the humans, the innocent and naive mannequin accepts bribes in the form of money and prostituted wives and daughters offered by the competing capitalists attempting to avert a strike. Involved in a duel with one of the gentlemen over a point of honor involving his wife, the mannequin hero leaps out the window, leaving the humans to finish the shooting among themselves.

Beneath the overt narrative of class warfare leading to Marxist revolution is Jasieński's hidden theme of the reign of fashion and the interchangeability of man and mannequin. Humankind is malleable, subject to remodeling, and prone to replication. "They're all only wretched copies made in our image!" the Mannequins declare, convinced that humans are their clones. In a society in which copies are made of copies, image triumphs over substance.

The method of dialectical materialism favored by RAPP would be of less use to actors playing Jasieński's mannequins and their human replicas than a knowledge of art history. The puppet–human relationship was a popular motif in early twentieth-century European art. Mannequins entered the vocabulary of avant-garde imagery with Chirico, Carrà, and the metaphysical painters who sought a mysterious reality beyond the visible in the iconography of the tailor's dummy. Chirico's metaphysical mannequins gave intimations of the ontological mystery of human existence. The imagery of the tailor's dummies served as a metaphor for the isolation, loneliness, and anxiety of the human condition.

In Germany, under the influence of the Italian *Pittura Metafisica*, Grosz, Scholz, Schlichter, and the *Neue Sachlichkeit* painters, using the techniques of verism, gave Chirico's and Carrà's mannequins a social and historical context. The result was powerful social satire on the world of the Weimar Republic, with its cold, calculating capitalist predators, buying and selling sex, and their poor crippled, limbless, or dismembered victims. Jasieński's *Mannequins' Ball* has analogues with both the Italian metaphysical painting and the German new objectivity inspired by it. Jasieński's headless fashion-salon mannequins suffer from their own inanimateness and long for "human" movement and freedom, whereas his capitalists and industrialists are soulless, mechanized mannequins manipulating other puppets, including their own wives and daughters, in order to gain economic and political power. If Grosz had illustrated *The Mannequins' Ball*, his angry, sensual, and grotesque caricatures would have revealed other dimensions of Jasieński's play than are to be seen in Moor's cool, severe, and almost abstract figures.

Antecedents and analogues for Jasieński's mannequins can also be found in the rebellious robots in Karel Čapek's *R.U.R.*, Oskar Schlemmer's *Triadic Ballet* and the Theatre of the Bauhaus, and the Italian Futurist mechanical dances of Fortunato Depero and Ivo Pannaggi. Behind all of these lie Craig's Übermarionettes, E. T. A. Hoffmann and Léo Delibes's *Coppélia*, and Kleist's essay, "On the Marionette Theatre." Two Polish artists continued Jasieński's experiment with tailors' dummies: Bruno Schulz with the "Treatise on Mannequins" in *The Street of Crocodiles* (1934) and Tadeusz Kantor with the "Theatre of Death" manifesto and *The Dead Class* (1975).

The Mannequins' Ball could never be performed in the Soviet Union of the 1930s. Its brand of high-spirited theatricalist satire, reveling in the glamor of rotten capitalist luxury, had long since been denounced as "Foxtrot communism." In 1923 Meyerhold's production of Alexei Faiko's *Lake Lyul* was condemned for presenting an appealing picture of the decadent West through its cosmopolitan imagery of "high life": hotels, bright lights, advertisements, and fancy evening clothes. Nouveaux riches NEPmen, their overdressed wives and mistresses attended the performances as if they were going to the latest Parisian fashion show. It is not surprising that Meyerhold hoped to stage Jasieński's play or that he was never able to; stylistically and ideologically it was out of step with the new era in Soviet culture.

The Mannequins' Ball was first performed in 1933 in Czech at E. F. Burian's experimental Theatre D34 in Prague where it found a proper home for its grotesque and playful fantasy. The stage design was by the Czech constructivist artist, Antonin Heythum. In Poland Jasieński had to wait until the thaw of 1956 to be rediscovered. *The Mannequins' Ball* was translated into Polish by Jasieński's fellow Futurist Anatol Stern and published in the theatre journal *Dialog*, in 1957, the year of its Polish premiere in Katowice, directed by Jerzy Jarocki, who twenty years later staged the first Russian production in the USSR. In 1974 at the Ateneum in Warsaw Janusz Warmiński directed an extremely successful production of *The Mannequins' Ball* that went on tour to both Western and Eastern Europe, including Moscow and Leningrad. Jasieński's "mannequins" finally triumphed over their persecutors.

The Polish premiere of *The Mannequins' Ball* in Katowice, 1957, directed by Jerzy Jarocki, stage designs by Wiesław Lange

Scenes from Janusz Warmiński's production of *The Mannequins' Ball*, stage design by Krzysztof Pankiewicz, at the Ateneum in Warsaw, 1974

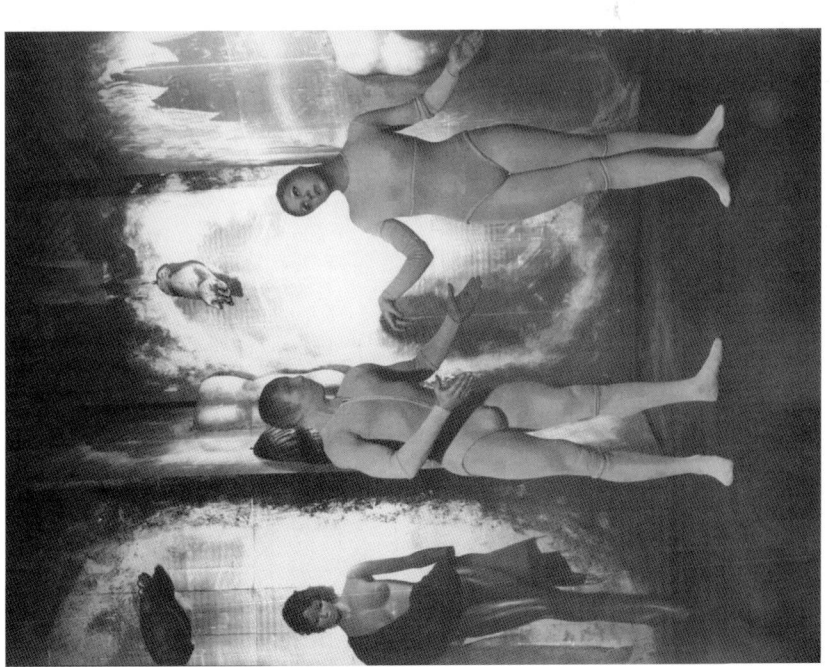

Scenes from Janusz Warmiński's production of *The Mannequins' Ball*, stage design by Krzysztof Pankiewicz, at the Ateneum in Warsaw, 1974

Sources for the Chronology and Introduction, with a Note on the Translation

Complete documentary evidence about Jasieński's arrest, imprisonment and execution (based on KGB archives recently made available) appears in Krzysztof Jaworski, *Bruno Jasieński w Sowieckim Więzieniu: Aresztowanie, wyrok, śmierć* (Kielce: Wyższa Szkoła Pedagogiczna im. Jana Kochanowskiego, 1995). Other accounts of Jasieński's life and career that I have drawn upon include Anatol Stern, *Bruno Jasieński* (Warsaw: Wiedza Powszechna, 1969); Zbigniew Jarosiński, ed., *Antologia Polskiego Futuryzmu i Nowej Sztuki* (Wrocław: Ossolineum, 1978); Janina Dziarnowska, *Słowo o Brunonie Jasieńskim* (Warsaw: Książka i Wiedza, 1978); Nina Kolesnikoff, *Bruno Jasieński; His Evolution from Futurism to Socialist Realism* (Waterloo, Ontario: Wilfrid Laurier University Press, 1982). Jasieński's play and its context are discussed in Harold B. Segel's *Pinocchio's Progeny: Puppets, Marionettes, Automatons, and Robots in Modernist and Avant-Garde Drama* (Baltimore: Johns Hopkins, 1995). Information about Dmitri Moor appears in Stephen White, *The Bolshevik Poster* (New Haven: Yale, 1990).

The translation is based on the Russian text of *The Mannequins' Ball* published in Moscow in 1931 with Lunacharsky's Introduction. Because there is no extant original or definitive text, I have also made use of Anatol Stern's Polish version of 1957 and the anonymous English translation that appeared in 1931 in *Literature of the World Revolution*, which, although often unidiomatic, inaccurate, and prolix, captures the period flavor of the work.

Elizabeth Swain, Irina Miller, Jane House, and David Willinger provided invaluable help with the translation, and Kei Hibino discovered the information about the unsuccessful attempt to stage *I Burn Paris* in Japan.

The introduction and chronology, as well as Lunacharsky's introduction and Moor's woodcuts and some of the production pictures, originally appeared in *Slavic and East European Performance*, Volume 17, No. 1 (Spring 1997).

Program illustrations by Jan Młodożeniec for the 1974 Ateneum production

Introduction by Anatolii Lunacharsky to the 1931 Moscow edition of *The Mannequins' Ball*

Bruno Jasieński is not afraid to use the latest artistic devices. Bold constructions, fantasy unrestrained by improbability, overt satirical tendentiousness, the emotive power of indignation that bursts forth from time to time like a flame – these are the things that he has accustomed us to in his previous works, such as *I Burn Paris* and *The Community Affair* [a dramatic version of his poem, *The Lay of Jakub Szela*, published in Russian as *The Galician Jacquerie*].

Not long ago a controversy raged in our literature and literary theory as to whether the proper style of proletarian literature is psychological realism, or whether the proletariat is better served by free stylization, hyperbole, and caricature utilizing techniques of the placard rather than those of the "naturalistic" picture.

The answer, obligatory for every Marxist-Leninist, that the style of the proletariat should be based on dialectical materialism in no way resolves the problem posed since it is easy enough to prove that both psychological realism used in a certain way and sharp political constructivism can go hand in hand with the dialectical-materialist method.

I do not know if at the time of those controversies Bruno Jasieński belonged to one or the other camp, or whether like me and many other writers he realized that the controversy was groundless because each of these methods represents a different side of a single proletarian style, a different kind of weapon of a single proletarian writers' army. In any case, in his brilliant comedy *The Mannequins' Ball* Jasieński in practice came down on the side of the fantastic that is both artistic and tendentious.

"Isn't it mysticism to depict a ball given by headless mannequins who have gathered together in one place from all the workshops in the city in order to enjoy movement?" Of course, a critic who asked such a question would be subject to universal ridicule.

Everyone understands that this does not reek of the mystical, but that the author has adopted a well-defined literary device that is imbued with the fantastic.

But another question might be posed: is this kind of fantastic necessary? Couldn't these same events and character types be presented in their natural circumstances in a realistic comedy?

We answer – it is completely possible.

But the comparatively scant material which in this instance Jasieński provides for the concrete characterization of his bourgeois and his socialists gains immeasurably by being shown to us in an unexpected mirror that unrealistically distorts proportions, but perfectly throws into relief those traits of the represented phenomena that the author wished to show us as vividly as possible.

We may likewise ask ourselves whether the impression is not weakened by the various inconsistencies and numerous absurdities in the situations resulting from the fantastic premise. In point of fact, the headless mannequins and the headless leader talk, although they have no mouths, they see although they have no eyes, etc. It would be possible to multiply such "malicious" questions about the physiology and psychology of the wooden mannequins or the decapitated human being who runs around without a head, almost as though nothing had ever happened.

But all this, of course, is trivial nit-picking. One must have enough inner freedom to accept all this fantastic bizarreness, just as the Greeks accepted a similar motley masquerade in the plays of their Aristophanes. The business of the director and of the actor's art is not only to eliminate

Russian premiere of *The Mannequins' Ball*, Chelyabinsk, 1976, directed by Jerzy Jarocki

the various discrepancies of the distinctive fairy-tale world created by the author's playful, yet at the same time malicious imagination, but also to extract a large number of interesting scenic effects from the fresh material given them in a drama that takes place between humans and mannequins. Once you have accepted the mirror of the fantastic held up by the author, you will grasp how curiously, originally, delectably, and sarcastically it reflects the "bourgeois-socialist" world, accurately targeted by the joyous feathery arrow let loose by Bruno Jasieński which he calls *The Mannequins' Ball.*

Translated by Daniel Gerould

Dmitri Moor: Illustrations for Bruno Jasieński's *Mannequins' Ball*.
1. Act I, Scene 1. Mannequins in a Parisian Fashion House give a ball.

THE MANNEQUINS' BALL

A PLAY IN THREE ACTS

DRAMATIS PERSONAE:

MANNEQUIN 1 (*male*)
MANNEQUIN 2 (*male*)
MANNEQUIN 3 (*male*)
MANNEQUIN 4 (*male*)
MANNEQUIN 5 (*male*)
MANNEQUIN 6 (*male*)
MANNEQUIN SIZE 46 (*male*)
MANNEQUIN SIZE 48 (*male*)
MANNEQUIN SIZE 50 (*male*)
MANNEQUIN 1 (*female*)
MANNEQUIN 2 (*female*)
MANNEQUIN 3 (*female*)
MANNEQUIN (*female*) IN A FUR CLOAK
MANNEQUIN SIZE 40 (*female*)
DEPUTY PAUL RIBANDEL (*Leader*)
MONSIEUR ARNAUX – *automobile manufacturer*
ANGÉLIQUE ARNAUX – *his daughter*
LEVASIN – *automobile manufacturer*
SOLANGE LEVASIN – *his wife*
DEVIGNARD – *banker* (*Banque de France*)
DELEGATE 1
DELEGATE 2
GENTLEMAN 1
GENTLEMAN 2
GENTLEMAN 3
GENTLEMAN 4
GENTLEMAN 5
GENTLEMAN 6
LACKEY 1
LACKEY 2
POLICE COMMISSIONER
MANNEQUINS AND GUESTS

The action takes place in Paris.

ACT I

A salon in one of the first-class fashion houses in Paris. Muffled sounds of a jazz-band are heard – the tango. Pairs of Male and Female Mannequins whirl about the stage. The Mannequins are headless; where their heads should be, there are rods.

They dance for a moment. Then the music dies down. The dancing couples disperse about the stage, many of them disappear into the adjacent rooms. At the front of the stage MALE MANNEQUIN 1 *walks arm in arm with* FEMALE MANNEQUIN 1. FEMALE MANNEQUIN 1 *fans herself with a huge ostrich feather.*

SCENE 1

FEMALE MANNEQUIN 1: What a joy it is to move, to whirl in a dance, to grow drunk with motion! Can you imagine a greater torture than being compelled to remain motionless, like a rock, for years on end? Only humans are capable of such cruelty! Really, I'm surprised I haven't totally forgotten how to move my legs. During those long months of absolute immobility it sometimes seemed to me that I'd grown rooted to the floor forever and that I'd never be able to detach myself from it. For this one night I was ready to give up the rest of my life. To move! To glide through space! To feel sweet weariness in the joints of my hands and feet! To bend and to unbend them! Can there be more complete happiness? I hate to think that this night will pass, that dawn will come, and that I must once more be turned into an immobile statue. The mere thought of it is enough to drive me mad. (*Clutches her partner's arm.*) Listen, 42, why, strictly speaking, can't we give balls like this more often? Why must we wait for carnival? Why shouldn't we get together every night?
MALE MANNEQUIN 1: Impossible. You know perfectly well we're tied to these premises. We wouldn't have music anywhere else. The owner of the fashion house on the first floor, to whose music we're dancing, gives a ball only once a year.
FEMALE MANNEQUIN 1: Is that really so important? Couldn't we get along without the music?

7

MALE MANNEQUIN 1: Of course we could, but where? At my boss's place it's unthinkable. You have no idea how difficult it was for me to get away today. The boss never leaves the workshop unless there's someone to watch it. One of the apprentices always spends the night there. You have to wait until he falls asleep to be able sneak out. But to bring so many guests there – is that really conceivable? They'd wake everybody up!

FEMALE MANNEQUIN 1: A human being's no obstacle. As a last resort, we can always kill him.

MALE MANNEQUIN 1: He'd make a racket. The humans would come running, nothing good would come of it. The humans would start being afraid of us. We'd be nailed to the floor forever. We must act with extreme caution, if we don't want to lose the last shred of freedom that's still left us. We've no place to meet. And it is not only at my workshop, there are watchmen everywhere – at Barclay's, at Sulky's, at Alba's, at H. Esders' and at the ladies' fashion salons too.

FEMALE MANNEQUIN 1: That's right. And at our place, particularly at carnival time, they work nights. They're finishing the ball gowns for the customers. They don't leave us alone for a minute. Last year during all of carnival it wasn't possible to arrange a single thing.

MALE MANNEQUIN 1: If it hadn't been for the strike at your atelier, nothing would have worked this year either. It was lucky for you that the whole work force went out on strike, and that the boss refused to make any concessions. Last year, at just the same time, our employees went out on strike too, but there were so many rush orders that the boss immediately agreed to raise wages so there wouldn't be any work stoppage. We gained nothing by it.

FEMALE MANNEQUIN 1: So we'll be nailed to the floor once again, perhaps for years on end. After tonight, now we've tasted the joy of movement, it will be even more painful…

(*A band starts up. The couples begin to dance.*)

MALE MANNEQUIN 1: Let's not poison tonight's happiness with thoughts of future suffering. We should enjoy the moment. (*Embraces his partner.*)

(*They dance off and disappear upstage.*)

SCENE 2

MALE MANNEQUIN 2: (*Rhythmically moving along the footlights with* FEMALE MANNEQUIN 2.) Well, how about it? Are we dancing again tomorrow? It would be inexcusably stupid to pass up such an opportunity. Surely your atelier will be empty for a few nights. Who knows how many years will go by before we have such a chance again!

FEMALE MANNEQUIN 2: (*In a melancholy voice.*) Which of us will live a few years longer? Fashions change so quickly nowadays! There's a rumor flat-chested figures won't be in vogue next year. Women with well-developed busts are coming back into fashion again. If that's true, then we'll all be tossed on the scrap heap next year.

MALE MANNEQUIN 2: Well, in that case what will they do with the flat-chested women? You know, almost all women are flat-chested nowadays! Will they go on the scrap heap too? And where will they get the other kind? Humans are not made as quickly as we are. Size 42 once told me all about it.

FEMALE MANNEQUIN 2: Quite likely some women will end up on the scrap heap too. I heard our proprietress say that about a lady customer from Kleber Avenue. But with humans, it seems, it's done a bit differently. After that I often saw this customer come and order new clothes for herself. Anyhow, I certainly don't think all flat-chested women will be discarded. Women can be remodeled. They say there are even special institutions or factories where they are completely remade. Depending on the fashion, they get chiseled down or have missing parts glued on. Apparently it pays. We don't get remodeled. It's not profitable. A new mannequin is cheaper. In that respect you males are luckier than we are – in your case fashions change less frequently, you live longer than we do. You'll last at least until the next ball…

MALE MANNEQUIN 2: What's keeping you from arranging the next ball for tomorrow? So what if there is no music? We'll get along without it! We must seize the opportunity. A few days more, and the strike will be over.

FEMALE MANNEQUIN 2: I am afraid it's already over. I heard the proprietress telling the manageress that starting tomorrow morning there'd be an entirely new staff of girls. Not one of the former seamstresses will be taken back. The proprietress said that new ones are coming by the score, begging for work. Starting in the morning everything most likely will go back to the way it was before. The nights will be devoted to finishing up the dresses. We shan't be able to arrange anything more this season…

(*The couple dances off and disappears upstage.*)

SCENE 3

MALE MANNEQUIN 3 *enters, carrying under his arm a Male Mannequin in a frock coat, who instead of legs has a rod.* MALE MANNEQUIN 3 *puts him against the wall.*

MALE MANNEQUIN 4: (*Addressing* MALE MANNEQUIN 3.) Hi there, 44! What's wrong with 42? Did they run out of legs? Did you have to drag him under your arm?

MALE MANNEQUIN 3: I'll say they were in short supply! They sent only three pairs of legs for our entire atelier. We somehow managed to come up with hands, but only ladies' hands. (*Shows one of his hands.*) But there weren't enough legs for him to get his. The poor guy had been so looking forward to this evening, got all spruced up, and then crash. His legs didn't come, and try to get around that. He begged not to be left behind, but to be taken along; said he'd be happy to stand in the corner and watch the others walking about and dancing. Made me feel sorry for him. I hoisted him up on my back and lugged him here. Let the poor guy stand there and look on. He'd be miserable all alone in the empty workshop. Maybe an extra pair of legs will turn up here?

MALE MANNEQUIN 4: That's a joke! No chance of that. Half our workshop had to stay behind, they didn't have anything to walk on. And what a lot of trouble there was with hands! They say there aren't any men's hands in all of Paris. Evidently the humans began to suspect something and hid them from us. We collected a few ladies' hands from glove shops and manicure parlors. Don't even mention feet – the hosiery shops have only ladies' legs. The shoemakers did have a few men's feet, but not enough to go around. I myself had to take ladies' legs, or I wouldn't have been able to get to the ball. (*Shows his feet in ladies slippers with high heels.*) I was in agony for a whole hour until I broke them in.

MALE MANNEQUIN 5: (*Who up till now has kept silent, breaks into the conversation.*) You can't even imagine all the trouble we've had organizing tonight's ball. Legs literally falling off from tiredness. You know, there aren't many of us complete mannequins – with arms and legs – and our numbers are dwindling every year. We were removed from the display windows of all the elegant shops a long time ago, now we're only kept in stores that sell all kinds of cheap trash. We have been crowded out by the mannequins with heads. And with that gang you won't come to any sort of understanding. They're so proud that humans put ceramic heads in their own image on their shoulders that they refuse to have anything to do with us. They are delighted to see the idlers hanging round the display windows and gaping at them for hours. So delighted that they make high and mighty faces and stick their noses up in the air. They repudiated us long ago. The entire job of organizing this ball fell on us. All evening long, divided into groups, we dashed about the city as though possessed, collecting all the arms and legs that were to be found. There were no more. You may take my word for it.

MALE MANNEQUIN 4: Let's go! The band has struck up. We'll get our fill of standing still: tomorrow, the day after tomorrow, whole years on end. But tonight I do not wish to remain motionless for even one second. I am going to dance.

(*They disperse.*)

SCENE 4

MALE MANNEQUIN 6: (*Moving rhythmically along the footlights with* FEMALE MANNEQUIN 3.) Who taught you to dance so beautifully? One would think you do nothing else all day long.

FEMALE MANNEQUIN 3: I learned by watching others. Our girls in the workshop – they're called mannequins too – walk like that when they model dresses for the customers. I watch them every day. I've had plenty of time to learn!

MALE MANNEQUIN 6: I don't believe there's anything to be learned from humans. I've seen more than enough of all those dandies who frequent our workshops. They're all only worthless copies made in our image! I feel like bursting out laughing when I look at those twisted monstrosities. They desperately want the clothes that suit us to perfection to look equally good on them. And so they're irritated when everything that fits us like a glove puckers and wrinkles on them. These freaks force the apprentices to slave away at night and use cotton padding for what they naturally lack, vainly attempting to make their figures look like ours. I simply can't understand why our clothes should be given to them. No matter what you do, on them everything will always look ghastly. And to think that that pack of apes whose only aim in life is to resemble us and try to equal us, to think that those monkeys are able to walk about and travel around from morn till midnight wherever they please, while we are compelled to spend the rest of our days stuck on a rod!

FEMALE MANNEQUIN 3: You're being unfair and because you're angry you're exaggerating. It's not true they imitate us so slavishly in everything. For instance, they wear heads which we don't.

MALE MANNEQUIN 6: Yes, their shoulders support those shapeless empty pumpkins they call heads. They fit them as wretchedly as do their clothes. I don't know, perhaps for some of them heads have a certain function to perform, but most of those parasites use them solely as props for their ridiculous stove-pipe hats. Now really, would any of us ever wear such a contraption?

(*Noise off stage.*)

SCENE 5

Pushing through the dancing couples, there appears on the stage a FEMALE
MANNEQUIN IN A FUR CLOAK. *The scarf wrapped around the rod creates
the perfect illusion of a head. The couples stop dancing. The* FEMALE
MANNEQUIN IN A FUR CLOAK *starts to unwrap the scarf. Everybody
gathers around her.*

MALE MANNEQUIN 3: What happened? Why didn't you take off your
   things in the hall?
FEMALE MANNEQUIN IN A FUR CLOAK: He's coming here... He's
   after me...
MANNEQUINS: Who?
FEMALE MANNEQUIN IN A FUR CLOAK: A human.
MANNEQUINS: What human? Where did a human come from?
MALE MANNEQUIN 4: Tell us clearly and quickly.
FEMALE MANNEQUIN IN A FUR CLOAK: A human... A man... He's
   coming here after me... He ran into the courtyard.
MALE MANNEQUIN 3: What human? Where did he come from?
FEMALE MANNEQUIN IN A FUR CLOAK: You see... I ran all the way
   from Cherlitte's. The woman on the night watch kept on fiddling and
   fussing about, and I had to wait until she fell asleep. That's why I am
   late. I wrapped myself up in this scarf so I wouldn't look different from
   the women in the street, and I ran here. It's not far. No more than ten
   houses. I hadn't even gone a few steps when some man accosted me.
   You see, he took me for a woman. He kept after me and insisted on
   escorting me. I began to walk faster. He followed me. I ran. He didn't let
   up. And while running, he kept spouting all kinds of nonsense, that
   I had beautiful little feet, that in his whole life he had never seen anything like them, that I shouldn't be cruel, and other things like that, half
   of which I didn't even understand. I wanted to throw him off the track
   and run away; I turned into a side street, but he grabbed me round the
   waist. I barely tore myself away. I ran round the block so as to double
   back. But he kept after me, not letting me get a step ahead of him. He
   was running and blabbing. I had no more strength left to run. I dashed
   into this building and saw that he was running after me. I rushed up the
   stairs, slamming the door behind me. When I came up here, I heard him
   opening the door down below. He'll be here any minute. What shall I do?
FEMALE MANNEQUINS: (*Frightened.*) What shall we do?
MALE MANNEQUIN 5: Lock the door immediately, let no one in!

(*At this very minute a* HUMAN *wearing an overcoat, a white scarf around his
neck, and a top hat appears at the door. General tumult. Then everyone comes to
a standstill.*)

SCENE 6

HUMAN: (*Runs in, stops in astonishment a few steps away from the door. Stares in amazement at the Mannequins. After a moment of silence.*) Excuse me ... But ... But I don't think I'm drunk ... Two or three small glasses of port ... No, I can't be drunk.

MALE MANNEQUIN 5: Well, there's no choice. (*To the* MANNEQUINS *who appeared at the door behind the* HUMAN.) Shut the door! Don't let anyone else in!

(*Two Mannequins lock the door behind the* HUMAN. *One of them hides the key in his pocket. They station themselves at either side of the door, their arms crossed. The Female Mannequins, frightened, crowd together in the opposite corner of the stage. Two Mannequins lock the door on the right side of the stage and station themselves as guards as the first pair did. Silence.*)

HUMAN: (*Ex ... excuse me ... Be so kind as to explain to me, please, what all this means. Is it a masquerade? (*Looks cheered, as if he had just hit upon a startling explanation. Visibly relieved.*) Well, yes, of course, it's a masquerade. I guessed it right off, at the first glance. An original idea ... Hee-hee ...

(*General silence.*)

HUMAN: (*Stops laughing.*) It certainly is original! A mannequins' ball ... And the costumes, hm, ... and the costumes are quite original too ... Hee-hee ...

(*General silence.*)

HUMAN: (*Continues*) Ladies and gentlemen, I have disturbed you without meaning to. Please forgive me. I mistook the door. Instead of the left door I opened the right one. The doors look absolutely identical ... And ... I ... didn't notice the name-plate ... Absentmindedness ... Hee-hee-hee ... Please, forgive me. I won't disturb you any longer. (*Turns and wants to leave by the door through which he had entered. Notices the Two Mannequins who block the way. He is at a loss.*) Eh ... eh ... Permit me, gentlemen ... I won't disturb you ...

(*Silence.*)

MALE MANNEQUIN 5: (*Sternly*) What shall we do with him?
MALE MANNEQUIN 4: We can't let him out now, that's clear.
MALE MANNEQUIN 6: Not now, not ever.
MALE MANNEQUIN 3: We've no choice, he's got to be killed.
MALE MANNEQUIN 2: Wait, my friends, this is a serious matter, it can't be decided in such an off-hand way. We have to look at it from all

Dmitri Moor: Illustrations for Bruno Jasieński's *Mannequins' Ball*.
2. Act I, Scene 8. Deputy Paul Ribandel, Leader of the Socialist Workers Party, intrudes
and is sentenced to death.

sides, and only then can a verdict be reached. I propose we immediately convene a court to settle this question.

MALE MANNEQUIN 6: We have only one night at our disposal, and are we to waste it deliberating what to do with this idiot? To my mind, the matter is clear – we can't let him go. And we can't keep him locked up either. Well, then? ...

MALE MANNEQUIN 1: Such matters can't be settled at one fell swoop; 46 is right, let the court decide.

MANNEQUINS: That's right! Let the court decide.

HUMAN: (*Addressing the Mannequins at the door, attempting to push them aside and open the door.*) I beg your pardon, gentlemen, but I'm in a terrible hurry. I'm expected elsewhere. I have no time for joking.

ONE OF THE MANNEQUINS: (*Grabs him by the shoulders and seats him on a chair by the wall.*) Sit!

(*Two Mannequins sit down on the two chairs on either side of the* HUMAN.)

MALE MANNEQUIN 3: Now we really can't afford to waste any time. It's a shame to let the night slip through our fingers. Have the court convened immediately.

MALE MANNEQUIN 2: Who will make up the court?

MALE MANNEQUIN 6: As usual. In keeping with our customs, the case will be heard by the larger sizes.

MALE MANNEQUIN 1: How many members should we elect?

MALE MANNEQUIN 5: Four will be enough; three judges and the prosecutor. What are the largest sizes we have here today?

MALE MANNEQUIN 2: 44, 46, 48, 50.

MALE MANNEQUIN 6: A table! We'll need a table.

MALE MANNEQUIN 1: A table and four chairs.

(*Two Mannequins place a table and three chairs in the center of the stage. The fourth chair is set to one side. The large-size Mannequins occupy their places and begin to confer in a whisper.*)

MALE MANNEQUIN 50: (*Stands up.*) I hereby declare the session of the court open. Colleague 44 will begin the prosecution.

(*The Mannequins move closer. Only the* HUMAN, *his guards, and the legless Mannequin remain near the left wall.*)

MALE MANNEQUIN 50: Colleagues, the case, which you have instructed us to examine, is as difficult as it is serious. A human has appeared at our ball. He came here uninvited, to spoil for us these few hours of freedom which we have won for ourselves with such difficulty. If this human returns to his fellow humans, the city will immediately learn of our ball. The humans, who have deprived us of legs so that we cannot move, will, on learning of our trick, hasten to rob us even of this last chance and nail us to the floor forever. Permitting this would mean sentencing ourselves to imprisonment for life. The human who has recklessly intruded on our ball must not be allowed to leave here alive. (*Sits down.*)

MALE MANNEQUIN 46: (*Addressing the* FEMALE MANNEQUIN IN A FUR CLOAK.) Number 40, have you anything to say on this matter?

FEMALE MANNEQUIN IN A FUR CLOAK: I've already told you everything. That human accosted me in the street. Followed me all the way. Ran in here after me. The rest you've seen for yourselves.

MALE MANNEQUIN 46: You don't have anything to add?

FEMALE MANNEQUIN IN A FUR CLOAK: No.

MALE MANNEQUIN 46: Has any one of the colleagues anything to say about the defendant personally?

MALE MANNEQUIN 1: I have.

MALE MANNEQUIN 46: Go ahead.

MALE MANNEQUIN 1: I know him personally. He's the same size as I am. He wears my suits. At this very moment he's got my tail-coat on. You can check it yourself. His right sleeve is half a centimeter shorter than his left. I recognized him as soon as he came in. He's the Leader, one of my boss's chief customers.

LEADER: (*Jumping up from his seat.*) Excuse me …

(*The Mannequin Guards place their hands on his shoulders, the* LEADER *sinks submissively into the chair.*)

MALE MANNEQUIN 50: The accused does not have the right to speak. (*Addressing* MALE MANNEQUIN 1.) What did you say? Leader? Is that his name?

MALE MANNEQUIN 1: That's what my boss calls him when he's out of sight. But when he's talking with him, he calls him "Monsieur le Deputé." I assume it's some kind of title. When they talk to one another, all the humans use honorifics.

MALE MANNEQUIN 48: Don't you know anything more about him?

MALE MANNEQUIN 1: He has sloping shoulders, and his coats are padded with cotton. He wears a black silk corset. He tries on each of his suits three times and always finds fifteen things wrong with them. When he says good-bye, he shakes hands with the apprentices. The boss dances around him on his hind legs and says he's a big shot. The apprentices cuss him for all they're worth and behind his back call him a "socialist chloroformist." He orders five suits each season, all of genuine English worsted, and once every four years a plain corduroy suit – without even trying it on. The boss sends for this fabric specially from the "Samaritaine" department store. Our boss wouldn't have accepted such an order from anyone else, because the material is too cheap. But for him he makes an exception, although he charges him as much as for any other suit. The boss treats it as a "special order," making the apprentices work overtime, and he says: "You'd better hurry, or the Leader won't have anything to wear for the election meetings."

MALE MANNEQUIN 50: What else can you say about him?

MALE MANNEQUIN 1: I might add it's not the first time he's spoiled our fun. During the last carnival he drove our entire workshop crazy on account of his tail coat: he claimed it didn't fit right in the waist. Three apprentices sweated over his tail coat all night long. As a result not one of us could get away to our ball at "Philippe et Gaston's." And now he's spoiled all our fun again.

MALE MANNEQUIN 50: All right, you may sit down. Anyone else have anything to say about this case?

(*Silence.*)

MALE MANNEQUIN 50: The Prosecutor has the floor.

MALE MANNEQUIN 6: (*Standing up.*) Gentlemen of the jury! In the light of all that has been said by the preceding speakers, there is very little left for me to do, but to summarize the opinion of the court and reach the only possible conclusion. Strictly speaking, the very fact that a representative of our oppressors, of those who have been inflicting so much pain and suffering upon us, burst into our ball would be sufficient to justify our dealing with him in the harshest manner. An act of legitimate self-defence, our sentence must at the same time also be an act of protest against this gang of parasites who have forced us to serve them. Imitating us, slavishly copying every line of our flawlessly harmonious forms, these humans, despite all their efforts, have still not been able to make themselves look like us in all particulars. What distinguishes them from us is the bump they wear on their shoulders. I demand that this brazen-faced wretch be rendered harmless and therefore propose that as a protest against this whole gang we amputate the useless excrescence on his shoulders. I demand that his head be cut off. (*Sits down.*)

(*The* LEADER *makes desperate gestures.*)

MALE MANNEQUIN 50: (*Stands up.*) The court is retiring to deliberate. The sentence will be pronounced in a few minutes.

(*The court retires. The Mannequins break out into loud conversation. They surround* MALE MANNEQUIN 6.)

SCENE 7

VOICES (*Interrupting one another.*)
– Cut off his head!
– By all means! But what with? We'd need a knife!
– Best would be with a hatchet.
– Yes, but where can we get one?
– If I'd known, I'd have brought one with me from our kitchen …
– Who could have foreseen this?
– Can't you find something sharp?
– Maybe he's got something in his pocket? Humans like to carry all kinds of sharp objects about with them.

LEADER: (*Jumping from his seat.*) Gentlemen! Stop your joking. Try and understand; I'm expected elsewhere. I'm already late for the ball at Monsieur Arnaux's.

MALE MANNEQUIN 4: What's he saying?

LEADER: At Arnaux's, the automobile manufacturer. Surely, you've heard of him? I'm not going for my own amusement, it's a very serious matter. Tomorrow a strike is going to break out in the automobile industry. Try and understand, gentlemen, that as leader of the workers party I can't waste even a minute. I'm asking you, let me go. I'll gladly spend an evening with you some other time, only not now. Your little joke is really wonderful and clever, but everything is well and good at the proper time. Now that you know who I am, you must realize that jokes that go beyond certain limits cease to be clever. Please let me go immediately.

(*Muttering is heard among the Mannequins.*)

MANNEQUINS: Silence! The court is coming!

(*The court enters and silently takes places at the table.*)

SCENE 8

MALE MANNEQUIN 50: (*Stands up, speaks solemnly.*) We, the judges of this court, having examined the case from every possible angle, have decided on the following: the human here present, known as the "Leader," is condemned to have his so-called head cut off. Given the lateness of the hour, the sentence must be put into effect forthwith. The prosecutor and one of the members of the court have volunteered to carry out the sentence. (*Turning to the crowd of Mannequins.*) Clear a space and make the necessary preparations. The sentence must be carried out within five minutes, and then the ball, which has been interrupted by the arrival of the prisoner, will be resumed.

(*The court rises and mingles with the crowd of Mannequins. The Female Mannequins clap their hands with joy.*)

VOICES: Faster! Faster!

(*Several Mannequins remove the table and the chairs, clearing the center of the stage.*)

VOICES: All right, but what will we cut his head off with? Where will we get a sharp object? We can't manage without a knife.

(*An uproar at the door to the right.*)

VOICES: Step aside! Make way!

(MALE MANNEQUIN 6 *enters carrying a huge pair of tailor's scissors. A buzz of amazement mingled with delight.*)

VOICES: Scissors! We've got scissors! We'll do it with scissors!
MALE MANNEQUIN 5: (*Making his way through the crowd.*) Step aside. Step aside.

(MALE MANNEQUIN 6, *carrying the scissors, and one of the Mannequin-Judges, carrying a heavy flat iron, advance to the center of the stage. They place the open scissors so that they rest with one ear and one edge on the floor.* MALE MANNEQUIN 6 *holds the upper ear of the scissors.* MALE MANNEQUIN 3 *holds the upper edge of the scissors. The* MANNEQUIN-JUDGE *stands holding the flat iron in readiness.*)

MALE MANNEQUIN 5: (*To the* MANNEQUIN-GUARDS.) Bring him over here!

(*The* MANNEQUIN-GUARDS *grab the* LEADER *by the arms and drag him to the middle of the stage toward the open scissors.*)

LEADER: (*Desperately trying to free himself. The* MANNEQUIN-GUARDS *pull his coat off.*) Let me go! Stop this nonsense! This is an outrage! I'll call the police! (*Defending himself, he pulls with all his might the arm of one of the* MANNEQUIN-GUARDS. *The arm remains in the* LEADER's *hands. Thunderstruck, he lets go of the arm. The arm falls clattering to the ground.*)

(*The* MANNEQUIN-GUARD *bends down, picks up his arm, and, in the most casual manner, starts to re-attach it.*)

Dmitri Moor: Illustrations for Bruno Jasieński's *Mannequins' Ball*.
3. Act I, Scene 8. Deputy Ribandel has his head cut off with a pair of giant scissors struck
with an iron.

LEADER: In the name of the Father, the Son and the Holy Ghost! What does this mean?

(*Several Mannequins throw themselves on him and drag him toward the scissors.*)

LEADER: (*Terrified*) Let me go! Stop this masquerade! Now I understand it all! It's a political plot! You've lured me here to compromise me. If you don't release me immediately, I'll bring it up before the Chamber of Deputies tomorrow! Let me go! Police! ... Police! ...

(*Two Mannequins push him to his knees, adroitly shoving his head through the blades of the open scissors.*)

MALE MANNEQUIN 6: Swing away!

(*The* MANNEQUIN-JUDGE *lifts the flat iron and brings it down full force on the top blade of the scissors. The severed head rolls across the floor.*)

LEADER: My head! My ministerial head!

(*Jumping after it, he tries to seize hold of his rolling head. The Mannequins drag him off to one side.*)

LEADER: (*Breaking loose.*) My head! You've stolen my head! (*Circling back, he runs out through the right door.*)
MALE MANNEQUIN 5: Grab him – he'll run away!
MALE MANNEQUIN 43: Without his head, he can run wherever he wants. Let him jabber from now till doom's day, no one will ever believe him. They'll think he lost his head on a drunken spree. Who'll take that gibberish of his seriously?
MALE MANNEQUIN 5: Away with the scissors. On with the ball.

(*Several Mannequins carry off the scissors and the flat iron. Some of the Mannequins have already started dancing.*)

MALE MANNEQUIN 2: (*Picks up the* LEADER's *head and, examining it carefully, turns it in his hand.*) And what shall we do with the head?
MANNEQUINS: Yes, that's right! The head! What shall we do with the head?
MALE MANNEQUIN 1: Give it to me.
MANNEQUIN-JUDGE: But why to you? Give it to me! I cut it off, so by rights it belongs to me.
MALE MANNEQUIN 3: What did you cut it off with? With the flat iron? We cut it off with the scissors. And who held the scissors? I did! The head belongs to me.
MALE MANNEQUIN 6: Big deal – he held the scissors! Anyone could have held them. But I found those scissors under the table in the

workshop. Without the scissors you couldn't have cut off his head at all. So who does the head belong to? Obviously, to me.

MALE MANNEQUIN 4: No, it doesn't! It belongs to me. I was the one who stuck it between the blades of the scissors.

MALE MANNEQUIN 44: Comrades, let's not quarrel among ourselves, time is flying. To avoid contention over ownership of the head, I suggest we throw it in the waste-basket.

MALE MANNEQUIN 2: Why throw it away? Let's cast lots! The one who wins gets the head.

VOICES: That's right. Let's cast lots.

MALE MANNEQUIN 1: The female mannequins won't take part in the drawing – what do they need a male head for?

MALE MANNEQUIN 6: Of course.

MALE MANNEQUIN 2: All right, let's begin. Who has a box of matches?

MALE MANNEQUIN 3: I saw a box of matches by the looking glass.

MALE MANNEQUIN 5: Here it is.

MALE MANNEQUIN 2: Hand it over. How many of us are there? We have enough. I'm breaking off the tip of one of the matches. Now, pay attention! I'm tossing the matches up in the air. Catch them. Whoever gets the match without the tip wins the head. One, two, three! (*Throws the matches up in the air.*)

(*The Mannequins catch the matches, hurling themselves on the floor and creating a melee.*)

MALE MANNEQUIN 1: (*Shouting*) I've got it! Here it is! Without the tip!
MALE MANNEQUIN 2: Let's see!

(MALE MANNEQUIN 1 *shows the match.*)

MALE MANNEQUIN 2: Right. You've won. Here's the head, take it.

(MALE MANNEQUIN 1 *takes the head, examines it, goes over to the mirror.*)

MALE MANNEQUIN 6: What do you need it for? What will you do with it?

MALE MANNEQUIN 1: (*In front of the mirror, tries on the head. Setting it on the rod, he claps it down with the palm of his hand. Looks at himself amorously in the mirror. Turns to the other Mannequins.*) You know, it's not bad!

FEMALE MANNEQUIN 1: Just like a human. If I hadn't seen you put it on myself, I'd swear you were the Leader.

MALE MANNEQUIN 1: (*Strutting about and looking in the mirror with evident self-satisfaction.*) Fits me to perfection!

MALE MANNEQUIN 7: (*At the back of the stage.*) There's a wallet lying here on the floor. The Leader must have lost it when he was struggling with us.

(*The Mannequins pass an elegant, monogrammed wallet from hand to hand, examining it with great interest.*)

MALE MANNEQUIN 1: Show me! (*He takes the wallet, opens it, and examines the contents.*) Money... Visiting cards... (*reads*) Paul Ribandel, Deputy... A photograph. Another photograph. Still another... All naked women... A railway pass. A bill. Another bill. Another bill. Two from Paquin's, and one from "Philippe et Gaston's." (*Reads*) "One evening gown, one riding costume, twelve ladies' undergarments." (*He puts everything back into the wallet; from another compartment he takes out a membership card, reads.*) Membership card – the League for the Protection of Human and Civil Rights. A check-book. Another membership card. (*Reads.*) The French Socialist Party, the parliamentary faction... (*pulls out another card, reads.*) An invitation. "Monsieur Arnaux has the honor of inviting Monsieur le Deputé Paul Ribandel to a ball that will take place on Thursday, January 17, at eleven P.M. Paris. January 12. Champs Elysées 17." (*Holds the card in his hand.*) Aha, this is the invitation to the ball at the auto manufacturer's to which our Leader was going in such a hurry. (*Suddenly strikes his forehead with his hand.*) I'm going!
MANNEQUINS: (*Dumbfounded*) Where?
MALE MANNEQUIN 1: Where? Did you all think I won the head to stay here with you? To wait for the first rays of dawn to steal back to the workshop? To tremble for fear that the boss or the apprentices might have noticed something? Once more to turn into a puppet on a stick? Day in and day out to keep trying on suits that are not being made for me? To wait patiently in the hope that within a year or two, or even ten, another occasion might arise for me to be able to gather together all the missing limbs and run off into the city for a few hours? No! I'm no such fool! I've had it! This sort of life is stifling me! This is the end! I won the head! Do you understand? A human head! A passport enabling me to roam the whole world over. To go wherever I please, whenever I please! A key that opens all doors for me. I'm going! I'm off and running! Coat! Gloves! Top-hat!
MANNEQUINS: Wait! Where are you off to?
MANNEQUIN 1: (*Already at the door.*) Au revoir! Enjoy yourselves! I'm expected at Arnaux's. I'm off to a ball with humans!

Curtain.

Dmitri Moor: Illustrations for Bruno Jasieński's *Mannequins' Ball*.
4. Act II, Scene 1. Devignard, a financier, attends a ball at the mansion of car manufacturer Arnaux and discusses the threatened strike.

ACT II

Foyer in the mansion of the manufacturer Arnaux. Upstage a wide glass door through which a ballroom filled with dancing couples can be seen. On the left side a window looking out onto the garden, and to the back a door. On the right side a door leading to the vestibule. Large soft armchairs, sofas, tables, palms. In the right corner a knight in armor. Music off stage – a tango.

SCENE 1

ARNAUX *and* DEVIGNARD *come out from the ballroom.*

ARNAUX: (*Offering* DEVIGNARD *his cigarette case.*) Genuine Turkish cigarettes, imported from Constantinople.

(*They light their cigarettes.*)

DEVIGNARD: By the way, persistent rumors kept circulating on the stock exchange today that there's going to be a strike in your plants tomorrow. Apparently you won't be able to fill the order you've accepted on time. Your stocks have been dropping precipitously. Tomorrow morning if the rumors about the strike prove to be true, I'm afraid your stock is likely to drop still lower ...

ARNAUX: The rumors will be proved false.

DEVIGNARD: So much the better ... (*Pause*) If a strike does break out, your position won't be enviable. I have not the slightest doubt that Levasin will immediately dump a bunch of your shares on the exchange in order to set off a panic. You should be prepared.

ARNAUX: There won't be any strike.

DEVIGNARD: I'd be very glad ... But I've heard it's already been declared. Perhaps I was incorrectly informed?

ARNAUX: Only the Communists have decided on a strike. The majority of the workers in my factory belong to the Reformist Trade Union, and they don't take orders from the Communists. Without the participation of the Reformist Union, any strike in my place is doomed in advance. And the Reformist Union won't join in the strike.

DEVIGNARD: Are you sure of that? At the present moment the political situation is such that, under strong pressure from below, the Reformist Union won't be able to keep out of the strike unless it's willing to lose its authority. They say sentiment in favor of a strike among the workmen is quite strong.

ARNAUX: (*Ironically*) I see you've got firsthand information.

DEVIGNARD: You know how it is – you mingle with the people, you can't help hearing things. I mean, the Banque de France ought to be a little bit better informed about what's going on. Anyhow, your affairs interest me personally. You made a pretty risky move. To cut the workers' wages by almost five francs a day at such a tense moment, when a strike is brewing, takes a lot of courage...or capital. Still, fortune favors the bold. Nothing would make me happier.

ARNAUX: I see they've managed to infect you with a bit of pessimism. I heard Levasin came to see you today and that you were in conference with him for an hour and a half.

DEVIGNARD: In conference? That's an exaggeration. Let's simply call it a little chat, a friendly little chat. You know that for a long time now I've had just as cordial relations with him as with you.

ARNAUX: I can imagine all the things he's accusing me of.

DEVIGNARD: Well, it's not quite that bad...Of course, he isn't especially grateful to you. After all, you did snatch an order amounting to half a billion right from under his nose. Nowadays such orders aren't to be found lying in the streets.

ARNAUX: I should think not. He has only himself to blame. Had he made a lower bid, the order wouldn't have slipped through his fingers.

DEVIGNARD: Don't you see, making a low bid is easy enough, but the real trick is fulfilling it. If a strike breaks out at your factory tomorrow, it may lead to a strike in the whole metallurgical industry.

ARNAUX: I've already told you there won't be any strike. The Reformist Union will come out against it decisively. The Communist instigators will continue to be an insignificant minority. Do you need proof? All right! You can convince yourself with your own eyes. I'm expecting Deputy Paul Ribandel to come to the ball tonight. As you know, he's the Leader of the Socialist Party, with whom we came to a firm agreement about this yesterday. This very day the Reformist Union will issue a proclamation against the strike. Do you still have any doubts?

DEVIGNARD: I never had any. I know you to be an experienced businessman and I'm sure you wouldn't take any risky step unless you'd covered your rear. You say Ribandel's coming here tonight? (*Pulls out his watch.*) It's already past two. Doesn't it seem strange to you that he hasn't showed up yet? I know that Ribandel's fanatically punctual. Don't you think that in the meantime something may have happened to change his original plans?

ARNAUX: That's impossible! (*Glances nervously at his watch.*) I'm surprised myself that he's not here yet. Something must have detained him. Party affairs, most likely. He's got a head on his shoulders! If he doesn't get a ministerial post at the next change in the government, I'll put my arm on the block. You may rest assured that once he's given his word, he'll come for sure. You'll see the kind of face Levasin makes when he meets Ribandel here.

DEVIGNARD: Well, let's rejoin the ladies. People will begin to suspect we're here discussing financial affairs. (*As they are passing through the door, he turns to* ARNAUX.) A propos, as for that five million you need, you understand, in the event of a strike our bank won't be able to give it to you. However, we'll talk about this later. (DEVIGNARD *goes to the ballroom. At the door, he bumps into* ANGÉLIQUE ARNAUX.)

SCENE 2

ANGÉLIQUE: (*To* DEVIGNARD) Ah, gentlemen, why are you off in a corner all by yourselves? Business, always business. At least during carnival couldn't you forget it for a while?

DEVIGNARD: Business? What an insulting suspicion! Would any of us dare to discuss business in the presence of beautiful women? We were just talking about hunting. Toward the end of the month Levasin intends to arrange a big hunting party with greyhounds. I hope you'll honor us with your company.

ANGÉLIQUE: He has just invited me. He even went so far as to offer me his best horse. By the way, he asked me where you'd disappeared to. I left him in the smoking room.

(DEVIGNARD *leaves.*)

SCENE 3

ARNAUX *mops his forehead with a handkerchief.*

ANGÉLIQUE: Why are you in a bad mood, dad? Was your conversation with him unpleasant?

ARNAUX: (*Looking nervously at his watch.*) I can't understand why the Leader isn't here yet. What can have happened? I'm afraid that swindler Levasin has already managed to sniff him out today. He's turned Devignard against me too. The old miser twists this way and that like a pennant in the wind.

ANGÉLIQUE: Yes, it's quite unpleasant, especially now you need him so.

ARNAUX: I should say so! Devignard is the Banque de France. Without the five million the Bank has promised me I won't be able to make the next payment of wages this Saturday. Do you realize what that means?

ANGÉLIQUE: But if there isn't any strike, the bank won't have any grounds for refusing you the money. Yesterday you came to an agreement with Ribandel about the position his union is taking, didn't you? So what's wrong now?

ARNAUX: What's wrong is that I'm afraid he's changed his mind. How else can we explain his absence? Levasin is ready to stand on his head to keep us from coming to an agreement. I am afraid he's already done a lot of harm. He's spreading rumors right and left that a strike in my factories has definitely been decided on. I've got to refute those rumors and reassure Rosenthal and the Banque de France. It's absolutely essential for me that the Leader appear at my ball. (*Pause*) If he comes, you must be very attentive to him. You can help me in this matter. Understand? You can even permit him some slight liberties. However, that's your own feminine affair, and I don't wish to interfere. Ribandel is known to have a weakness for the fair sex. And he's always been very attentive to you. You should try to bind him to us as closely as possible. We'll need that man again on more than one occasion.

ANGÉLIQUE: I understand, I understand … Don't worry. I'll do whatever's necessary. I can't even say that he totally displeases me. True, he looks dissipated, but he seems to be a real connoisseur of women …

ARNAUX: Well, that's your affair, my child. I refuse to get mixed up in it. I repeat that to me this is very important.

ANGÉLIQUE: And will you make me a present of a new car? One of those eight cylinder models with interior controls you're planning to put on the market in the near future?

ARNAUX: I'll give you anything you want. (*Looks at his watch.*) What's going on? He's still not here.

ANGÉLIQUE: When he arrives, you'll call me, won't you? I'm going to dance. (*She stops at the door and laughs.*) You know, Levasin is making a play for me. He even invited me to look at his collection of Chinese engravings. (*Runs out, laughing.*)

ARNAUX: (*Alone, impatiently heads for the telephone.*) Elysées 47–82. That's right.

(*Enter a* LACKEY.)

LACKEY: (*Announces*) Monsieur le Deputé Paul Ribandel.

(ARNAUX *slams down the receiver and rushes off to meet* RIBANDEL.)

SCENE 4

Enter the MANNEQUIN-LEADER, *timidly looking about the entire room.*

ARNAUX: (*Runs over to him.*) Well, at last! You've kept us waiting, dear Leader. (*Shakes his hand.*) I understand, I understand – duties, party

Dmitri Moor: Illustrations for Bruno Jasieński's *Mannequins' Ball*.
5. Act II, Scene 3. The Mannequin-Leader, who has put on Ribandel's head and assumed
his place, checks his appearance before arriving at Arnaux's ball.

affairs. Of course, of course... What would those poor workers do without their Leader? But surely, we, the non-proletarians, are entitled to at least a little of your time? One in your position, one who personifies the union of the two forces that rule the world – labor and capital – while devoting himself unstintingly to labor, must not forget about filthy capital either. (*Pulls him toward a chair.*) Please, sit down, dear Leader. (*Points to the chair.*)

(MANNEQUIN-LEADER *takes a seat, looking embarrassed.*)

ARNAUX: Before we go into the ballroom, let's settle our business. All right? Business first, and then pleasure. That motto of yours has always been mine as well. Things have reached such a pass that we cannot procrastinate any longer. The Communists in my plants have already declared a strike. No doubt you know all about it? Further delay is impossible. The Reformist Trade Union, motivated by a deep understanding of what is good for the workers, must come out decisively against the strike. At the present moment, when the country is going through a severe economic crisis, we must all make sacrifices. And unless the workers are willing to give up a few francs a day, my plant will have to shut down. Given the present level of unemployment, they are all likely to find themselves thrown out on the streets, swelling the hordes of the unemployed. I think it's better to lose five francs than one's entire wages. It won't be difficult for you to explain that to your workers, will it? Harmony in industry and the resulting prosperity of the entire country are based on a mutual understanding of the interests of the worker and the employer. In this respect, your party has given proof of tireless efforts and of truly civic understanding of the country's good. This in no way means that I am in principle opposed to strikes. If the manufacturer really makes big profits because of favorable conditions, why shouldn't he raise the workers' wages? But there is a difference, a great difference, between rational strikes and harmful strikes, strikes whose sole purpose is to undermine the foundations of the existing order. I well know the tremendous difficulties with which your party must struggle if it is to paralyze the growing influence of the Communists, who receive gold from Moscow. As a grateful member of this society for whose benefit you gentlemen are working so valiantly, I make bold to present you with this modest sum to be put at your disposal. Let it be used to fund the first rational strike under the guidance of your party. (*Looks furtively at the door, tears a check out of his checkbook, and hands it to the* MANNEQUIN-LEADER.)

MANNEQUIN-LEADER: (*Takes the check hesitatingly.*) Yes … But …

ARNAUX: No "but's," dear Leader! No "but's"! Haven't I the right as a citizen of this country to work for its rational development and to contribute, though in a modest fashion, to the improvement of the working conditions of those who give all their time and all their energy to increasing the good of society? Well, not another word about it. (*Rises*) Now let's join the guests. I haven't the right to deprive them of your company. My daughter would never forgive me for it. (*Takes the* MANNEQUIN-LEADER *by the arm and guides him to the door leading to the ballroom. The door of the ballroom suddenly opens and* ARNAUX *and his guest are met by* ANGÉLIQUE, DEVIGNARD *and* LEVASIN.)

SCENE 5

ANGÉLIQUE: (*At the door, to* LEVASIN *and* DEVIGNARD.) Don't you believe me? Let's ask daddy. (*Notices her Father with the* LEADER. *To the* LEADER.) At last! (*Offers him her hand.*) We'd lost all hope of seeing you here tonight. (*Reproachfully*) How could anyone be so late?

ARNAUX: (*Casting triumphant glances at* LEVASIN *and* DEVIGNARD, *he takes the* LEADER's *arm demonstratively.*) Duties, duties. (*Significantly, to* DEVIGNARD *and* LEVASIN.) At such a difficult moment people like our esteemed Leader must devote all their time to warding off the evil that is threatening the social equilibrium of the country.

(LEVASIN *and* DEVIGNARD *greet the* LEADER *ingratiatingly.*)

ANGÉLIQUE: Daddy, Monsieur Levasin doesn't believe I'm going to get an eight-cylinder car. He says you're not making them and that at the present time you can't produce automobiles of that sort. Tell him, please, so he'll stop contradicting me.

ARNAUX: (*To* LEVASIN *emphatically.*) Monsieur Levasin is mistaken. Now as never before I can produce any kind of car.

ANGÉLIQUE: (*To* LEVASIN) Well, what was I telling you? Who was right? You've lost the bet! (*To her Father and the* LEADER.) And what's more, the wager was to be set by the winner. You should be quaking with fear! Who knows what I may demand of you.

LEVASIN: Excuse me, I don't yet consider that I've lost. Humans are prone to error. The facts will speak for themselves. I'll admit I'm the loser only when you come to pick me up in your new car and take me for a round of golf.

(SOLANGE, LEVASIN's *wife, appears at the door to the ballroom.*)

SOLANGE: Gentlemen, is this some new kind of party game? Every chance you get you go off and hide in some corner! You're boycotting the rest of the company.

LEVASIN: (*To the* LEADER.) Do you two know one another? Monsieur le Deputé Paul Ribandel, this is my wife.

SOLANGE: (*Without any special interest, in a conventional manner.*) So pleased to meet you, I've heard a lot about you.

ARNAUX: Off we go!

ANGÉLIQUE: Monsieur Ribandel, you asked me for a tango, didn't you? (*Takes him by the arm and leads him to the ballroom.*)

(SOLANGE *sits down in an armchair, fanning herself with an ostrich feather.* ARNAUX *waits politely for* DEVIGNARD *to pass through the door first.*)

DEVIGNARD: (*At the door.*) By the way, about that five million, strictly speaking, the matter's settled. You can get it tomorrow. (*Exeunt*)

SCENE 6

SOLANGE: (*Alone with* LEVASIN.) Poor Frederick, you're circling around Mademoiselle Angélique like a cat around a saucer of cream, and she doesn't pay you the slightest attention. I'm truly sorry for you. If you want me to, I can help you. I'll have a talk with her. I don't guarantee success, but still it's somehow easier for a woman to approach another woman about such matters.

LEVASIN: You're talking nonsense. I need Mademoiselle Arnaux like a hole in the head. If you want to help me, help me along a different line: get the Leader hooked. Arnaux, evidently, twisted him around his little finger. They must have arranged to have the Reformists come out against the strike. Without their participation the strike in his factories is bound to collapse. And Arnaux will be in a position to fill the order on time and according to the stipulated terms.

SOLANGE: What business is that of mine? You're ridiculous. You bore me to death with your strikes and your socialists. You know all that leaves me cold. I wouldn't even lift my little finger for all that nonsense. I am willing to persuade the Arnaux girl to look on your advances with favor. But to get mixed up in any of those strikes… I wouldn't even dream of it.

LEVASIN: (*Irritated*) What's at stake here is not a strike, but the half a billion francs that Arnaux stole right from under my nose.

SOLANGE: But what business is that of mine? I hope you don't expect me in my old age to take your financial affairs and embarrassments to heart. Whether you steal half a billion from Arnaux or whether Arnaux steals half a billion from you – all that ultimately has nothing to do with me...

LEVASIN: (*Angrily*) It seems you'd even prefer that Arnaux stole from me.

SOLANGE: It doesn't make the slightest difference to me.

LEVASIN: I doubt that!

SOLANGE: You're in a bitter mood tonight, I see, and you insist on bringing up subjects you'd do better to avoid. All that's missing is for you to stage a jealous scene for my benefit. The role of a jealous husband would even suit you nicely. (*Laughs*) I'm going to burst... (*Laughs louder.*) Let's invite an audience. I'm not so selfish that I want to enjoy such an unusual show all by myself.

LEVASIN: I don't interfere in your affairs and I never have. I'm not much interested. I ask nothing of you in return other than that you don't interfere in mine either.

SOLANGE: Do I interfere? If I offered my help in your flirtation with the Arnaux girl, it was only because you started this affair from the wrong end. You're simply getting old. I wanted to render you a friendly service.

LEVASIN: Drop that stuff about the Arnaux girl! If I need her sometime, I won't hesitate to make use of your services. But right now I've got more important things on my mind. I stand to lose half a billion francs.

SOLANGE: My dear, if someone managed to steal such a sum right from under your nose, it only proves you're growing older and stupider every day. But why don't you steal it back from him?

LEVASIN: That's just what I intend to do.

SOLANGE: Well, go ahead, who's stopping you?!

LEVASIN: You can help me with this. I've never asked you for anything, although perhaps I have some right to do so. Because of your expenditures this past month I almost had to stop paying the workers' wages last week.

SOLANGE: My dear, a wife is an expensive luxury. It is about time you realized that.

LEVASIN: I don't ask you to make any sacrifices, all I want is for you to turn the Leader's head. You understand, you may even allow him some slight liberties. But that's your feminine business, and I don't want to interfere. The chief thing is to influence him so that he'll push his union into a strike at Arnaux's plant. You can see for yourself, the business is purely feminine and simple. I'm sure that if I didn't take such an interest in it, you'd have no objections to flirting with Ribandel. He really is an attractive male, his success with the ladies is phenomenal. The task, you see, is not a very difficult one.

SOLANGE: He's not my type. It's hardly worth the effort.

LEVASIN: It's not yet certain if you're his type! (*Teasingly*) When I intro-
duced him to you, he didn't pay you the slightest attention. Apparently
success with the ladies has spoiled him. Did you see how the Arnaux
girl was chasing after him? I sense that a rival like that would give you
plenty of trouble. After all, she's somewhat younger than you.

SOLANGE: Trying to goad me into action? How would you like to bet
that within two hours I'll have him twisted around my little finger?

LEVASIN: I have serious doubts about that.

SOLANGE: (*Aggressively*) A bet! Anyhow, let's forego the bet. You seem
to know my weak spot. I'll show you that ten ninnies like your
Mademoiselle Arnaux put together wouldn't come up to the heel of
my slipper! And besides, while it's true the Leader is not exactly my
type, I can't say that I altogether dislike him. True, he looks dissipated, but he has what you might call "it"! He must be impossibly
cynical. See, you've convinced me. After all, why not? (*Rises and goes
toward the door.*)

LEVASIN: Wait , you don't even know what you're to ask him for ... The
thing is ...

SOLANGE: I don't need you to teach me what I'm to ask for. I don't
intend to ask for anything for you. Ask for it yourself! (*Goes out.*)

(LEVASIN *is left confused and perplexed.*)

SCENE 7

The MANNEQUIN-LEADER *comes in through the door to the left, closing it
quietly behind him. For a moment he listens to hear whether he is being followed. He does not notice* LEVASIN *standing in the corner. He takes a handkerchief out of his pocket and wipes his forehead. Exhausted, he sinks heavily
into an armchair, fanning himself with his handkerchief.*

LEVASIN: (*Approaches him from behind.*) Worn you out, have they?

MANNEQUIN-LEADER: (*Jumps up from fright. Hastily hides his handkerchief in his pocket.*) Worn me out? No, what an idea!

LEVASIN: I can imagine how overworked you must be these days. The
country hasn't been in such terrible shape for a long time. Industry at
a standstill. Slump getting worse. Prices skyrocketing. It's no wonder
our workers are growing restless and demanding higher wages! You
think I don't understand them? I understand them perfectly. I would
have been the first to increase wages in my own factory if I had the

wherewithal. Orders are non-existent, production has to be reduced to a minimum. Then how could anyone raise wages? The best you can hope for is to pull through these hard times. And yet even at such a difficult moment, there are industrialists – don't have to look far, take our respected host, Monsieur Arnaux, for example – there are industrialists who deliberately set out to provoke the already aroused working masses. To cut today's wages! Tell me, isn't that a provocation? Isn't that an open challenge to the workers to strike? (*Pause.*)

MANNEQUIN-LEADER: (*Hurriedly*) Yes, yes, of course. (*Looks all around, as if searching for a door through which to slip away.*)

LEVASIN: I knew in advance that you could not fail to condemn such irresponsible conduct. Individuals like Monsieur Arnaux jeopardize the peace and security of the whole state. The socialist party must take a decisive stand against such adventurers, as it always has against all kinds of firebrands who recklessly place a lighted fuse next to a powder keg. A skillfully conducted strike called at the right time as a means of clipping the wings of high-handed individuals is the best method and a guarantee of real peace in industry and of a real union between efficient labor and humane capital. Wouldn't you agree?

MANNEQUIN-LEADER: (*As though awakening from a dream.*) Yes, yes, of course!

LEVASIN: You'll readily understand that if in Arnaux's case, your Reformist Union, instead of joining the strike, tried to hold the workers back, it would be making a huge mistake. In that case the Communists would seize the leadership of the strike, directing all the anger of the workers, whose sole object should be Arnaux, against your union. They'll claim you were allies of Arnaux and advocates of cutting wages. The unrest among the workers in Arnaux's plants is so strong that the strike will undoubtedly be successful anyway. In that case you would lose all the influence you now have in Arnaux's plants and in the entire district. The Reformist Union must join the strike, take the initiative into its own hands, and it must do so immediately, this very night, or else the Communists will beat you to it. What's your opinion?

MANNEQUIN-LEADER: My opinion? Yes, of course, of course.

LEVASIN: (*Rejoicing*) So the Reformist Union is joining the strike? Well, of course, it's clear as day! You must be surprised I'm even asking you such a question. Knowing the firm principles of your party, I never doubted it for a moment. (*With a rapid gesture pulls his checkbook out of his pocket.*) I'm aware of the great difficulties your party has to contend with in order to check the growing influence of the Communists. As a grateful member of this society for whose benefit you, gentlemen, are working so valiantly, I make bold to put this modest sum at your disposal, for the strike fund. (*Fills out a check and hands it to the* MANNEQUIN-LEADER.)

MANNEQUIN-LEADER: (*Takes the check hesitatingly.*) Yes ... but ...

LEVASIN: No "but's," dear Leader! No "but's"! Don't I as a citizen of our country have the right to be concerned for its rational development and to aid, though in a very modest way, in furthering the efforts of those who devote all their time and energy to the good of society? Really, let's not say another word about it!

(ARNAUX *appears at the ballroom door.*)

SCENE 8

ARNAUX: (*Notices the* LEADER *and* LEVASIN. *Unpleasantly surprised.*) Oh, the Leader's here! The ladies are asking for you.

LEVASIN: (*Caustically*) The Leader and I have just had a very interesting conversation about the current economic situation. It's amazing how we agree on so many points.

(*Enter* SOLANGE.)

SOLANGE: Is the Leader here?

ANGÉLIQUE ARNAUX: (*Enters through the left door.*) Isn't the Leader here?

(*Both notice the* LEADER *at the same time and approach him simultaneously.*)

SOLANGE: Leader, am I dancing the Charleston with you?

ANGÉLIQUE: Leader, did you ask me for the Charleston?

ARNAUX: I swear, you'll tear him to pieces.

SOLANGE: Leader, you told me to wait for you.

ANGÉLIQUE: Leader, you asked me for this dance.

LEVASIN: (*Ironically*) The only solution is to draw lots!

SOLANGE: Let the Leader decide for himself.

ANGÉLIQUE: Leader, did you ask me for this dance?

MANNEQUIN-LEADER: (*Embarrassed*) Really ... Of course ...

ANGÉLIQUE: Let's go. (*Pulls him by the arm.*)

MANNEQUIN-LEADER: (*Already following* ANGÉLIQUE, *to* SOLANGE.) Really ... it seems ... yes ... maybe ... the next ...

ARNAUX: (*Good-naturedly*) She dragged him off! Hee-hee! It's amazing the way women gravitate to him.

LEVASIN: He's a fascinating person! What keenness of judgment, what farsightedness, what cold-blooded calculation and decisiveness! All the qualities of a great politician.

ARNAUX: Indubitably, indubitably.

LEVASIN: I'm going back to finish my game of bridge. Wouldn't you like to take part in the next game? You'll find me with Devignard in the third room, to the left, behind the column.

ARNAUX: Unfortunately my duties as host deprive me of the pleasure of having you as my partner. I still have some orders to give. (*Goes to the right and says something to the* LACKEY.)

LEVASIN: (*Heading toward the door to the left, on the way remarks casually to his wife.*) By the way, you don't have to bother. I arranged it all myself. Anyhow, I see I managed better than you would.

SOLANGE: Idiot!

(LEVASIN *goes out through the left door.*)

SCENE 9

ARNAUX: (*Lights a cigarette; pause.*) What's this business deal you didn't manage to arrange for him?

SOLANGE: Don't be so inquisitive, you might – without even meaning to – eavesdrop on an intimate family secret.

ARNAUX: Family secrets don't interest me. What interests me much more is what your husband had to say to the Leader. I caught them by surprise. They were deep in some confidential conversation. He didn't mention it to you, did he?

SOLANGE: Will you stop pestering me about your dirty business deals! First it was one, and now it's the other! Go hang yourselves, both of you, with your half a billion. Cheat, do as you please, but don't annoy me. You know, that doesn't interest me.

ARNAUX: Of course, it doesn't have to interest you. No matter which one of us rakes in that half a billion, it all works out the same for you.

SOLANGE: How's that so?

ARNAUX: That's just it! Your thoughtlessness and habitual lack of any sort of consideration have driven me to despair. You don't know when and what one can allow oneself. Your last bill from the jeweller's went beyond all possible bounds. If you intend to carry on that way in the future, I'll have to shut down the plants and declare myself bankrupt.

SOLANGE: My dear, a mistress is an expensive pleasure. It's time you got used to it. By the way, I'm glad you reminded me, I have a small request to make of you. The day before yesterday Devignard and I were in Deauville. I played roulette and, as luck would have it, did pretty poorly.

ARNAUX: (*Incensed*) Well?

SOLANGE: I lost about one hundred and fifty thousand. I owe Devignard. I promised to pay it back within a week.

ARNAUX: Have you gone out of your mind! One hundred and fifty thousand?

SOLANGE: Believe me, it's the first time in my life I've ever had such rotten luck. Judging from that, I should have phenomenal success in love!

ARNAUX: And you imagine I'll pay that debt?

SOLANGE: I don't imagine, I'm sure. I've always considered you a gentleman, and I have no reason to doubt it now. You know quite well that I can't ask Levasin for the money. I used up my allowance from him three months ahead of schedule.

ARNAUX: You're joking, my dear! At the present time there's no point even talking about my giving you such a sum.

SOLANGE: What do you mean "at the present time"? You made half a billion.

ARNAUX: In the first place, I haven't made a franc yet; so far I've only got the order. And I still don't know if I'll be able to fill that order. Anyhow, just a moment ago I heard you say that my financial affairs didn't interest you and that you were absolutely indifferent as to who got that half a billion – Levasin or I.

SOLANGE: You take my words much too literally.

ARNAUX: In short, the payment of your debt depends wholly on whether the order stays mine or whether Levasin snaps it up. His whispering with the Leader disturbs me greatly. You could help me.

SOLANGE: Oh, I know, I know. All you want me to do is to turn the Leader's head, permit him some slight liberties, and persuade him to get the workers to strike.

ARNAUX: You've lost your mind! Just the opposite! He has to come out against the strike.

SOLANGE: Oh, the other way around? All right – let it be the other way around.

ARNAUX: You don't even have to pressure him into it. I already have definite guarantees. Try to find out, if you can, what Levasin was discussing with him and what their relations are. As Levasin's wife, you should find it easy. The Leader won't have any reason to hide it from you.

(*Both move towards the door leading to the ballroom.*)

SOLANGE: All right, all right, I'll do it.

ARNAUX: (*By the door.*) But don't get it mixed up. He may think you're trying to get something for Levasin. You may spoil the whole thing.

SOLANGE: Don't be afraid! The Leader is no fool. He'll understand immediately what I want from him.

Exeunt.

SCENE 10

A LACKEY enters through the door to the right, followed by two men. They are wearing dark suits, bright tan shoes, colored socks, flashy neckties, and bright silk handkerchiefs stick out of their lapel pockets. The first walks with self-assurance, the second more timidly, looking around in wonder, awkwardly hiding behind his back his rough hands which serve as evidence of his working class origins. Clearly he's imitating the first one in both clothes and gestures.

LACKEY: How shall I announce you?

DELEGATE 1: Ask to see comrade deputy Paul Ribandel in person, citizen, and tell him that the comrades from the union have come for instructions. Can you remember that? The comrades from the Metal Workers' Union have come for instructions.

LACKEY: Monsieur le Deputé Ribandel is in the ballroom and at the present time is not engaged in any business.

DELEGATE 1: Citizen, go and repeat what I told you. The comrade Deputy himself told us to look for him here at three in the morning and to have him come out into the vestibule. Just tell him the comrades from the Metal Workers' Union have come for instructions. Comrade Ribandel will understand.

LACKEY: You wait here. Don't go any further. (*Goes out through the door leading to the ballroom.*)

DELEGATE 2: (*To DELEGATE 1, enthusiastically.*) What a parquet floor! Eh? Feet just glide along all by themselves. Somebody not used to it could get his skull cracked.

DELEGATE 1: Oh, this is nothing! You should see the ballroom! Feet start dancing all by themselves! No mirrors needed, you can see yourself from head to toe.

DELEGATE 2: No kidding! Comrade, were you ever in a ballroom belonging to capitalists?

DELEGATE 1: Sure thing! Not here, not at Arnaux's place, I was at other peoples' places. As a matter of fact, I went on party business. (*Looks around, notices the armchairs; to the DELEGATE 2.*) Sit down! We're not going to wait around standing; after all, chairs were made to sit in.

DELEGATE 2: Somebody could come in.

DELEGATE 1: (*Sinks into a chair.*) So what if somebody does? Don't we have the right to sit down? Learn to respect your own party dignity, and then even the capitalist will, as a matter of fact, treat you with respect. He'll offer you a chair himself.

DELEGATE 2: (*Feels the chair, then sits down. Pleased with himself.*) These potentates of capital don't live half bad! Eh? A chair like this must cost a pretty penny!

DELEGATE 1: Under socialism every party member will, in point of fact, have a chair like that. Some already do now. It's the best proof that socialism is just around the corner. Do you think the Leader's apartment is worse than this one? No, sir! And he's not the only one! In case you didn't know it, social evolution, in point of fact, always works from the top down. Of course, it takes quite a while before it reaches the bottom. Only certain individuals are able to meet progress half way. In case you didn't know it, society, well, how can I explain it to you, is like a building. Different classes get to the top in different ways. The rich ones, the capitalists, travel to the top in comfort by elevator without even stretching their legs. For those who have no capital, but belong to the privileged classes, there are front stairs – wide and deeply carpeted. For the proletariat too, there are stairs, separate, but narrower – backstairs. Not many will fit on those stairs at the same time. Backstairs of that sort are, as a matter of fact, what our party is. The entire proletariat en masse cannot scramble up the staircase, but the cleverer ones will climb up step by step.

DELEGATE 2: With a head like that, Comrade Secretary will make it to the top.

DELEGATE 1: Anyone who has a head on his shoulders will make it to the top. You're still young, not long in the party, so watch your elders and learn. In case you didn't know it, for a beginner politics is like rowing. When you go rowing for the first time, your head starts spinning. You pull to the right, and you go to the left, you pull to the left, and you go to the right. It seems to you that everything's the wrong way round. Only when you adjust to it, do you begin to understand that to go in the direction you want to go, you have to pull in the opposite direction. At first, until you figure out this secret, everything will astonish you. If you start getting too clever, you're done for, you'll go to the bottom. The first thing in a political career is not to be astonished at anything and to watch what your elders do. Even if to you it seemed clear as day that that wasn't what was needed, keep your mouth shut and do as you're told. You'll understand later. Politics, pal, is a tricky business.

DELEGATE 2: Yes, but doesn't it sometimes happen that even high-up party workers make mistakes and take nasty spills? Then how can you tell what it is – a mistake or a political manoeuvre?

DELEGATE 1: Before a leader of that sort takes a spill, you'll be food for worms. You can rest assured that if such a leader takes a spill, it's because he has something to gain by it politically. When you've been in the party longer, you'll understand.

SCENE 11

LACKEY: (*At the door.*) Here, Monsieur le Deputé.

(MANNEQUIN-LEADER *enters, both* DELEGATES *rise precipitously.*)

DELEGATE 1: At your service, Comrade Leader. (*Offers his hand timidly.*)
MANNEQUIN-LEADER: (*Shakes his hand.*) Good evening.
DELEGATE 2: (*Also offers his hand timidly.*) At your service, Comrade Leader.
MANNEQUIN-LEADER: (*Shakes his hand.*) Good evening.
DELEGATE 1: We've come for instructions, Comrade Leader, as you ordered. It's three o'clock sharp.
MANNEQUIN-LEADER: For instructions?
DELEGATE 1: That's right! The Communists have already issued a proclamation calling for a strike. Here's a copy. Straight from the printing shop. (*Takes a leaflet out of his pocket and hands it to the* LEADER.) And here's the text of our appeal against the strike. (*Hands him another leaflet.*) No need to read it, Comrade Leader. The text is the same as always. All you have to do is sign it.
MANNEQUIN-LEADER: Y-y-yes … (*Unfolds the first leaflet and reads it aloud.*) "Comrades, the administration of the Arnaux plants, in utter disregard of the terrible conditions in which the workers live, is now cutting our already low wages by another five francs per day, thus exposing the workers' families to slow death by starvation. This step seems all the more contemptible when we realize that Monsieur Arnaux has just landed an order from abroad amounting to a half a billion francs. Arnaux's attempt, if it is crowned with success, will serve as an impetus for reducing wages in the entire metal industry. Comrades, the amalgamated union of metal workers, after closely studying the situation, has decided to call all of you to active resistance. This brazen provocation by an exploiter, drunk with power, must be met by the workers of all the plants with a one hundred percent strike. Workers of all convictions! To defend your elementary rights, you must join hands in the common struggle! Let us create a united front that will force the bloodthirsty capitalist sharks into submission! Down with capitalist exploitation! Give us our five francs back! Long live the

united front of the working class! Down with the dictatorship of the bourgeoisie! Long live the dictatorship of the proletariat!" (*After reading it, he folds up the leaflet. To the* DELEGATES.) Quite right! I'll sign immediately.

DELEGATE 1: Comrade Leader...you mean you'll sign our appeal? That's the Communist proclamation. Ours is the other one, the one you have there in your hand – against the strike.

MANNEQUIN-LEADER: But why bother with the other one, if this one is fine? The only thing is that perhaps they're asking for too little. A mere five francs. If those wages aren't enough to feed the workers and their families, then they should ask for more. Ten francs at least! Arnaux throws money around right and left. Why shouldn't he give them more?

DELEGATE 1: That...yes...But...in that case the workers in Levasin's plants will go on strike tomorrow and demand a raise too.

MANNEQUIN-LEADER: Let them. They'll have every right to! Why should they earn less?

DELEGATE 1: (*Perplexed*) In that case...if I understand you correctly, Comrade Leader...we're going out on strike too. And we're announcing a strike not only at Arnaux's, but also at Levasin's at the same time.

MANNEQUIN-LEADER: Certainly.

DELEGATE 1: And we're to print a proclamation with the same text as the Communists?

MANNEQUIN-LEADER: Why change it, if this one is fine? Just put ten francs instead of five.

DELEGATE 1: (*Increasingly perplexed.*) So we're demanding more than the Communists? That puts us at the head of the strike. Then we've got to issue a proclamation to Levasin's workers too. The same content, but with the appropriate changes? Did I understand that right?

MANNEQUIN-LEADER: Aha!

DELEGATE 1: Is that all you wanted to tell us, Comrade Leader?

MANNEQUIN-LEADER: Yes, that's all. Wait, I almost forgot. (*Pulls out his wallet and takes out the two checks.*) Take these checks, I got them from Arnaux and Levasin for the strike fund.

DELEGATE 2: Checks from Arnaux and Levasin? For the strike fund in their plants?

MANNEQUIN-LEADER: Aha! (*Still holds the wallet in his hands and suddenly notices Ribandel's money in it. Takes it out and hands it over to* DELEGATE 1.) Deposit this money in the fund too. It's Deputy Ribandel's money. Well, so long. They're waiting for me in there. I'm going to dance. (*He executes some fancy footwork and dances off into the ballroom.*)

SCENE 12

Both DELEGATES *stand dumbfounded for a moment. A long pause.*

DELEGATE 2: Pinch me, comrade! Either I'm dreaming all this, or I don't understand a single thing. No, it's no dream. He left us the checks, you're holding them in your hand! What's written there?

DELEGATE 1: (*Examines the checks.*) Two hundred and fifty thousand from Arnaux and two hundred and fifty thousand from Levasin. They're real honest-to-goodness checks. No doubt about it. And here's another ten thousand in cash.

DELEGATE 2: If you weren't right here, I'd swear I'd gone crazy. We're going out on strike at Arnaux's, we're reprinting the Communist proclamation, we're increasing their demands one hundred percent, we're declaring a strike at Levasin's plants, where until now no one even thought about striking. And to accomplish all this Arnaux and Levasin are handing out money. Makes your head spin!

DELEGATE 1: (*Scratches the back of his head.*) Too bad I didn't at least get the order from him in writing so that later on I couldn't be held responsible for the whole mess. Anyhow, you were a witness. He said it in your presence. There can't be any doubts about it. He spoke perfectly clearly. You heard it all, didn't you?

DELEGATE 2: Oh, I heard it all right, but I don't understand one damn thing about any of it. Either we've lost our minds, or he's gone crazy.

DELEGATE 1: (*Regaining his composure, now with the look of someone who has just worked something out.*) You imbecile! You can't figure anything out! Didn't I tell you that politics is a tricky business? Watch what your elders do and don't get too smart. If the Leader gives us precisely those instructions and not any others, it means he has some higher political considerations. I'm starting to understand what's up.

DELEGATE 2: (*In astonishment*) Do you really understand anything about all of this?

DELEGATE 1: If I tell you I'm starting to understand, it means I'm starting to understand. This is a clever political move – there can't be any doubt about that. Otherwise, as a matter of fact, why would Arnaux and Levasin give us money for it? The idea is to make a new and decisive move against the Communists. That way we beat them at their own game. It's easy as pie. In the first place, we take the leadership of the strike into our own hands, and secondly, we compromise the Communists for having asked for too little. Arnaux and Levasin give money for it, because it pays them good returns. It'll be easier for them to reach an agreement with us later. You still don't understand? Let's not waste time. We've got to act with lightning speed.

DELEGATE 2: (*Despairingly*) It looks as though I'll never make a politician.
DELEGATE 1: (*Near the door to the right.*) When you've been in the party as long as I have, you'll stop being surprised at anything whatsoever. I've had to solve tougher puzzles than those in my years in the party. Let's go. (*Exeunt*)

(*The* LACKEY *enters from the right, examines disapprovingly the place where the Delegates were sitting. Rearranges the furniture.*)

SOLANGE: (*Enters through the left door.*) Wasn't Monsieur Ribandel here?
LACKEY: Monsieur Ribandel was here a minute ago, Madame. He's gone back to the ballroom.

(SOLANGE *exits to the ballroom. The* LACKEY *leaves by the right door.*)

SCENE 13

Almost at the same time there appears at the left door ANGÉLIQUE ARNAUX, *pulling the* LEADER *by the arm.*

ANGÉLIQUE: Come over here. At least, it's quiet here. All those people wore me out. I'd like to rest from all that noise. Let's sit here. Oh, what a glaring light … it hurts one's eyes. (*Turns the switch, the salon is now in semi-darkness. Makes herself comfortable on the chaise longue, draws the* MANNEQUIN-LEADER *closer.*) I'm so tired … (*Leans her head on the* LEADER's *shoulder.*)
MANNEQUIN-LEADER: Shall I bring you a pillow? (*Rises*)
ANGÉLIQUE: (*Draws him back to his seat.*) Sit down. (*Nestles up against him.*) How strange you are! … It's true then, women simply bore you to tears?
MANNEQUIN-LEADER: Women? Bore me? Oh, no, not in the least!
ANGÉLIQUE: Don't deny it, we know you. Besides, it's common knowledge that the women won't give you a moment's rest. Even tonight, they won't let us be alone together for a minute. That unbearable Madame Levasin literally pulls you out of one's arms. She forces herself on you at every step. She has a pretty face, there's no denying that, but there's something vulgar about her, her mouth is too wide. I can't stand that type of woman. Does she please you?
MANNEQUIN-LEADER: Yes … she has a fairly nice figure, except that for a size 40 her hips are a bit too flat.
ANGÉLIQUE: How you take women apart piece by piece! You undress them with your first glance. In her case, however, you are quite mistaken. Her legs are too short. In a skirt, that's not visible, she wears her waist-line quite high. But if you see her without her clothes on, and

I'm sure you'll have a chance before long, you'll be convinced of it yourself. Besides, that woman engages in no form of sport, except love. And that's not conducive to the development of a good figure. She only plays golf, and that pretty poorly.

MANNEQUIN-LEADER: (*Confidently*) There aren't any perfectly built women. They've all got one flaw or another.

ANGÉLIQUE: You're trying to provoke me! I assure you, if there weren't so many people around, I'd prove to you that you're mistaken.

MANNEQUIN-LEADER: *You* would? ... (*Looks her over*) Size 38 small.

ANGÉLIQUE: How did you know?

MANNEQUIN-LEADER: It's my specialty ...

ANGÉLIQUE: That's amazing! In that case, when do you find time for politics? To know women the way you do you have to lavish lots of time on the subject.

MANNEQUIN-LEADER: You're exaggerating. Once you've had some practical experience ...

ANGÉLIQUE: But it seems you haven't told me your opinion. What flaws have you detected in me?

MANNEQUIN-LEADER: (*Examining her carefully.*) You have almost no bust. That's why your dress doesn't fit quite right.

ANGÉLIQUE: (*Offended*) Whaaat? You know, that's sheer impudence! (*Pulls her brassiere down impetuously and exposes her breasts, her back to the audience.*) Well? Are you still prepared to stand by your opinion?

MANNEQUIN-LEADER: (*Looks her over very dispassionately with the eye of a connoisseur, turning her about gently with his right hand and tapping her shoulder-blades.*) Your shoulder-blades stick out too much ...

(*The door of the ballroom opens wide, and* ARNAUX, DEVIGNARD *and* LEVASIN, MESDAMES *and* MESSIEURS *appear.*)

SCENE 14

ARNAUX: Why is it so dark in here? (*Turns the switch, lighting the stage brightly.*)

ANGÉLIQUE: Oh! (*Grabs the* LEADER *and hides behind him.*)

ARNAUX, DEVIGNARD, LEVASIN, MESDAMES AND MESSIEURS: (*In chorus*) Ah!

MANNEQUIN-LEADER: (*To* ANGÉLIQUE *imperturbably.*) You've torn your brassiere. You never should take your dress off so impulsively.

ANGÉLIQUE: (*Squeezing up against him.*) Quiet!

(MESDAMES *and* MESSIEURS *withdraw and go back again into the ballroom.*)

ARNAUX: It's just … that is … I meant to say …

ANGÉLIQUE: (*Calmly, fixing her dress.*) Daddy, it's about time you told the guests about our engagement. (*Buries her nails in the* LEADER's *hand.*)

MANNEQUIN-LEADER: You'll break my finger.

ANGÉLIQUE: (*In a whisper.*) Be quiet! One more word out of you, and I'll say that you forcibly ripped my dress off. I always considered you a gentleman.

ARNAUX: Yes, of course! I completely forgot. That is, I didn't forget … I only meant to do it later … But since that's what you want, we can do it right now. (*Turns to* LEVASIN *and* DEVIGNARD.) Monsieur Ribandel and my daughter … Just today we decided to announce it … That is, we're announcing their engagement.

LEVASIN: (*Caustically*) We saw. Better announce it to those who didn't see.

DEVIGNARD: (*Goes over to the* LEADER *and shakes his hand warmly.*) Congratulations!

MANNEQUIN-LEADER: (*Shakes his hand.*) At your service.

LEVASIN: (*Goes over and in his turn shakes the* LEADER's *hand.*) Congratulations! (*In a whisper.*) I hope you haven't forgotten our conversation?

MANNEQUIN-LEADER: Of course, everything's taken care of.

ARNAUX: (*To his daughter, embracing her.*) Let's go, my child; let's go, ladies and gentlemen. We have to announce this happy news to the guests.

DEVIGNARD: And raise our glasses to the health of the engaged couple.

(*Every one exits, except the* MANNEQUIN-LEADER.)

SCENE 15

The MANNEQUIN-LEADER *alone, examining his fingers.*

SOLANGE: (*Appears at the door to the left.*) You're here, all by yourself? That tigress Angélique has finally let you out of her clutches! It's the first time all night we'll be able to have a moment together alone. You know, I go for that cynical twist of your lips. The women must have been pestering you something awful?

MANNEQUIN-LEADER: The women? You know, they really have been chasing after me a bit. They won't give me a moment's rest.

SOLANGE: What conceit! But that's what I like about you. You know how to spurn women. I can imagine how that Angélique Arnaux must have been pestering you all evening. She never stops butting in.

She literally pulls you away from anyone else. She won't even let me be with you for ten minutes. She has a pretty face, no disputing that, but there's something fishlike about her. Not to mention that her mouth is too wide. Anyhow, you certainly must have noticed that yourself.

MANNEQUIN-LEADER: Just a moment ago Mademoiselle Arnaux said exactly the same thing about you.

SOLANGE: About me? What insolence! I can imagine how she painted my picture. That's an old trick used by provincial coquettes afraid of the competition. What other slander did she manage to tell you?

MANNEQUIN-LEADER: She said your legs are too short. She said that in a dress it's not visible, because you wear your waist line quite high.

SOLANGE: My legs too short?! The insolence of that ninny exceeds all bounds! My legs too short?! Well, what have you got to say for yourself? How did you answer her? Or are you of the same opinion?

MANNEQUIN-LEADER: As for your legs, I won't venture an opinion. I don't know. I just have the impression that for a size 40, you're a bit too flat in the hips. No woman is perfectly built. They all have their flaws.

SOLANGE: If there weren't so many people around, I'd prove to you right now, without any further delay, how mistaken you are.

MANNEQUIN-LEADER: Mademoiselle Arnaux tried to prove it to me too, but I stuck to my opinion.

(*The offstage orchestra plays a flourish.*)

SOLANGE: Are you trying to provoke me? Very well then! I don't give a damn about the people here! (*Quickly unbuttons her dress, with her back to the audience.*) Well, how about it? Do you still dare maintain your opinion?

MANNEQUIN-LEADER: (*Examines her with the eye of a connoisseur.*) Your hips are insufficiently curved. As for your legs, nothing simpler than to measure them. (*Gets down on his knees and begins to measure her legs with his hand from the hips down.*)

(*The door to the ballroom is flung wide open, and at the threshold there appear ARNAUX, DEVIGNARD, LEVASIN, ANGÉLIQUE, and a crowd of guests.*)

THE GUESTS: (*In a chorus*) Where is the fiancé?

SCENE 16

ALL PRESENT: (*Catching sight of the MANNEQUIN-LEADER on his knees before SOLANGE.*) Ah!

(*The sound of champagne-glasses breaking.* ANGÉLIQUE *lets go of her glass and faints.* ARNAUX *catches her as she falls.*)

MANNEQUIN-LEADER: (*Rises from his knees, slowly and calmly.*) Very
   flat hips!
SOLANGE: How dare you!
DEVIGNARD: A nice story!
LEVASIN: (*Pale, drawing closer to the* MANNEQUIN-LEADER.) What
   did you say?
MANNEQUIN-LEADER: (*Calmly*) Very flat hips.

(LEVASIN *takes a wide swing with his arm and strikes the* MANNEQUIN-
LEADER *on the cheek.*)

ALL PRESENT: Ah! (*They have all drawn together in a group. Only the*
   MANNEQUIN-LEADER *remains in the center of the stage.*)
MANNEQUIN-LEADER: Excuse me, but, strictly speaking, why?
ARNAUX: Monsieur le Deputé Ribandel, after all that has happened,
   I think there's nothing else for you to do but to leave my house.
MANNEQUIN-LEADER: (*Astonished*) Me?

(*Offstage the sound of doors being locked.*)

LACKEY: (*Appears from the right side. Stands at attention.*) Monsieur le
   Directeur!
ARNAUX: What's happened?
LACKEY: The Police Commissioner.

(*Enter the* POLICE COMMISSIONER *hastily through the right door.*)

POLICE COMMISSIONER: (*At attention, reports as though to someone of
   higher rank.*) My excuses, Ladies and Gentlemen, but circumstances
   admit of no delay. A strike has been declared in your plants, Monsieur
   Arnaux. The workers are trying to organize a demonstration. The
   square in front of your mansion has been designated as the meeting
   place. The Prefect of Police has sent a unit under my command to protect you and your guests. I've given orders to close all exits and
   entrances and not to permit anyone, under any circumstances, to
   leave, until the street has been cleared of demonstrators. Your guests
   will be forced to stay in your house until we receive further orders.

(*General tumult.*)

Curtain.

Dmitri Moor: Illustrations for Bruno Jasieński's *Mannequins' Ball*.
6. Act II, Scene 16. The police protect Arnaux and his guests from the strikers in the street.

ACT III

The same foyer in Arnaux's mansion. The stage is empty.

SCENE 1

The window in the left wall, looking out onto the garden, begins to shake as if someone were trying to open it. It is finally opened. The upper part of a headless body appears, and then the whole body. A human creeps into the foyer; he then brushes his clothes. This is the real LEADER, Paul RIBANDEL. The LEADER furtively approaches the door leading to the ballroom.

MANNEQUIN-KNIGHT: (*In knight's armor, until now absolutely motionless in the corner, suddenly stirs.*) Tsss!

(*The LEADER stops in astonishment.*)

MANNEQUIN-KNIGHT: Tsss! Where are you going? Are you crazy? Have you lost your way, or what? Humans live here. Beat it, or they'll see you.

(*The LEADER turns around, bewildered.*)

MANNEQUIN-KNIGHT: Where are you coming back from? Is our ball over? Were there lots of us? I planned to go, but I couldn't get away from here. Besides, in this shell I could hardly walk through the streets without drawing a crowd of gapers. And I wouldn't wish my worst enemy to dance in this kettle. I had to give up the idea. Well, how was everything there? Was the ball a success? Were there enough legs for everyone?
LEADER: (*In a rage.*) Shut up! I'm no mannequin! I'll show all of you! Cutthroats! Where is my head?
MANNEQUIN-KNIGHT: What head? What are you gabbing about? You've gotten drunk as a human.
LEADER: You don't know what head? The head you stole from me, you bandits. Just wait, I'll get you yet! (*Turns resolutely to the ballroom door.*)
MANNEQUIN-KNIGHT: (*Blocking the way by stretching out his arm.*) Don't you dare go in there! Have you lost your senses? They'll notice you. You'll get us all in hot water.
LEADER: (*In greater rage.*) Step aside!

(*A brief scuffle. The broken-off iron glove falls clattering to the floor. Enter the LACKEYS through the right door; they examine the room suspiciously. The MANNEQUIN-KNIGHT stiffens back into his former position.*)

SCENE 2

LACKEY 1: What's going on here?

LACKEY 2: (*To the* LEADER) Who are you, Monsieur? What are you doing here? Where have you come from?

LEADER: I am le Deputé Paul Ribandel; I must see Monsieur Arnaux immediately.

LACKEY 1: That's a good one! As it happens Monsieur le Deputé Paul Ribandel is here already. He's in the ballroom now. You'll have to be christened with another name.

LACKEY 2: And where did you dig up such a fancy costume?

LEADER: Is Deputy Ribandel here? Allow me to go in, I must talk with him immediately.

LACKEY 1: We just heard you say you were Deputy Ribandel, and now you want to speak with Deputy Ribandel. Seems you've got a screw loose: you've forgotten who you are.

LEADER: I am Deputy Ribandel, and I wish to speak to the impostor who's pretending to be me.

LACKEY 2: There's a funny guy for you! How did he get in here?

LACKEY 1: He must have climbed over the fence into the garden. Don't you see, the window is open.

LEADER: Look, I haven't a moment to spare! Announce me immediately to Monsieur Arnaux, or call Monsieur Arnaux out here.

LACKEY 2: First you want to see Deputy Ribandel, and then you want to see Monsieur Arnaux. Can't you make up your mind who you want to see? Run along and find your head so you can stick it under a water faucet. Maybe that'll help some.

LEADER: Let me pass immediately. How dare you speak to me in that tone!

LACKEY 1: Ho-ho-ho! How should we speak to you, Honored Count, since you refuse to tell us whom we have the honor of addressing?

LEADER: I've already told you. I am Deputy Paul Ribandel!

LACKEY 2: We've already heard that. Surely, Count, you must at least have some sort of a visiting card; without a visiting card we can't announce you.

LEADER: Unfortunately, I haven't any – they were stolen from me.

(*The* LACKEYS *roll with laughter.*)

LACKEY 1: They were stolen from him!

LACKEY 2: Just who stole them?

LEADER: I'm not obliged to give you an accounting! For the last time I ask you to tell Monsieur Arnaux that I'm here.

LACKEY 1: Hey, you better not cause a fuss! Go back down where you came from!

LEADER: Citizens, please understand, this is urgent … I have to see him about the strike that is liable to break out in Monsieur Arnaux's plant.

LACKEY 2: If that's the problem, there's no need to worry. Monsieur le Deputé Ribandel has already taken care of that down to the last detail. The strike will take place without your help.

LEADER: What do you mean? Did that impostor say something about it?

LACKEY 2: He sure did. It's all been settled. You can relax on that score. The delegates from the Metal Workers' union were here to see him. He gave them instructions without even waiting for you.

LEADER: Instructions? What kind of instructions?

LACKEY 2: He told them exactly what they needed to know. That Deputy of yours is a great guy. But at the last minute – no one knows why – he got way out of line and got smacked in the mug.

LEADER: That's impossible! You've all gone out of your minds! I must see Monsieur Arnaux immediately. I must clear it all up, understand? (*Wrestles with the* LACKEYS *who refuse to let him pass.*)

LACKEY 1: (*To* LACKEY 2.) What the hell are you gabbing with him for? He's a fine one to tell your stories to. Your tongue just keeps on wagging all by itself. Can't you see the guy is stewed to the gills? It's just asking for trouble later on.

LEADER: (*Shouting*) Let me by, let me by this minute!

LACKEY 1: Quiet, damn you! Make your racket out on the street. It's not enough for you to worm your way into somebody else's house, but just look at how you're carrying on here! (*Pushes the* LEADER *to the window.*) Get out while you're still in one piece. Or else I'll call the police. (*To* LACKEY 2.) Give the Count a hand!

(*They push the* LEADER *through the window.*)

LEADER: (*Already on the other side of the window.*) People, citizens, comrades, please understand …

LACKEYS: (*Pushing him out.*) We understand, we understand. (*They shut the window.*)

LACKEY 1: Nice guy, eh? First time in my life I've ever seen anyone that plastered.

LACKEY 2: Probably coming back from some masquerade. No shortage of guys who got pie-eyed wandering around the city in broad daylight unable to find their way home. That's what they have carnivals for.

SCENE 3

MANNEQUIN-LEADER: (*Enters through the door to the left. He is alone. Looks melancholy as he paces about the room. To the* LACKEYS *who are leaving.*) The door downstairs locked? Impossible to get out?
LACKEY 2: Absolutely no way, Monsieur le Deputé. Police orders not to let anyone out. Things are heating up in the streets.

(*Both* LACKEYS *leave through the right door. The* MANNEQUIN-LEADER *whistling plaintively, paces up and down the stage.* ARNAUX *comes out of the ballroom. At the same time* LEVASIN *walks in through the left door. Both start for the* LEADER, *but noticing each other they nonchalantly, slowly with studied absentmindedness, walk to the opposite door. Both whistling.*)

ARNAUX: (*To* LEVASIN *on meeting him.*) You didn't happen to see Devignard, did you?
LEVASIN: Devignard is playing bridge, the third room to the left.
ARNAUX: Thank you.

(*Walk in opposite directions pretending not to have noticed the* MANNEQUIN-LEADER. *Both reach the doors.*)

MANNEQUIN-LEADER: (*To* ARNAUX) Won't there be any more dancing?

(ARNAUX *stops in the doorway as if ready to answer.* LEVASIN *stops too.* ARNAUX, *upon noticing* LEVASIN, *does not say a word and walks out quickly.* LEVASIN *disappears through the opposite door.*)

MANNEQUIN-LEADER: (*Shrugging his shoulders.*) If not, then so be it ...

SCENE 4

GENTLEMEN 1 *and* 2 *enter from the ballroom and head toward the* MANNEQUIN-LEADER.

GENTLEMAN 1: Monsieur le Deputé Ribandel? We should like to offer you our services, if this privilege has not already been granted to somebody else.
MANNEQUIN-LEADER: Much obliged, but what kind of services do you mean?
GENTLEMAN 2: We offer ourselves as your seconds.
MANNEQUIN-LEADER: (*Interested*) What kind of seconds?
GENTLEMAN 1: As your seconds. In your duel with Monsieur Levasin.
MANNEQUIN-LEADER: Duel? What kind of duel?

GENTLEMAN 2: That's just what we do not know – whether you'll use pistols or swords. The choice of weapon belongs to you as the injured party.

GENTLEMAN 1: That is, we're ready to establish who really is the injured party – which in this case is a matter of dispute. When it's a question of a first degree offense, the seduced woman's husband who has given the offense does not have the right to choose the weapon.

MANNEQUIN-LEADER: What seduced woman are you talking about?

GENTLEMAN 2: (*Chuckling*) Hee-hee-hee! It's a technical term. In this case, it is Madame Levasin. A woman, as a person incapable of giving satisfaction, according to the code of honor, cannot be a seductress. She is always only the seduced woman, regardless of what the actual circumstances were accompanying the scene in flagranti.

MANNEQUIN-LEADER: What did you say?

GENTLEMAN 2: In flagranti. In matters of honor you may wholly rely on us.

GENTLEMAN 1: The Colonel is renowned in the best society as an authority in matters of honor and as an expert referee in the most intricate conflicts arising on this account. You may with absolute confidence entrust this case to him.

MANNEQUIN-LEADER: What case are you are talking about, gentlemen? What makes you think I intend to shoot at Monsieur Levasin or to run him through with a sword?

GENTLEMAN 1: Oh, we understand perfectly well that as a socialist you consider, and with good reason, duels as vestiges of feudalism. Nevertheless, in such cases this is the simplest and least troublesome way of settling these matters. In my opinion, it would be best to go through with the duel immediately, tonight, in any one of the secluded salons in Monsieur Arnaux's mansion. Two shots, two holes in the air – and the matter is settled. Relations between you and Monsieur Levasin will automatically revert to their former intimacy, to the greatest satisfaction of Monsieur Levasin, and, I assume I am not in error if I say, to your mutual satisfaction.

MANNEQUIN-LEADER: Excuse me, gentlemen, but I don't understand in the least why it's so important for you to force me to shoot Monsieur Levasin or why I actually have to do so? Is it because Monsieur Levasin slapped me, and you think I'm angry with him on that account? I'm not in the least angry, I assure you. Maybe you think it hurt me? Let me tell you a little secret: it didn't hurt at all. If Monsieur Levasin thought that he could cause me physical pain by striking me, he was only deceiving himself. And now I don't understand why in addition to everything else I have to take a shot at him.

GENTLEMAN 1: (*Chuckling*) Hee-hee-hee! Monsieur le Deputé is inclined to be jocular … We understand perfectly that as a socialist it's awkward for you to conform to our bourgeois prejudices. But in the best interests of both parties, this whole affair will never go beyond these walls. The point is not only that you should – permit me to use your witty expression – "take a shot at Monsieur Levasin," but also that – to paraphrase your expression – "Monsieur Levasin should take a shot at you." You can't deny him that pleasure!

MANNEQUIN-LEADER: What? I should agree to let Monsieur Levasin take a shot at me for his own pleasure? Never!

GENTLEMAN 2: I don't think you take the whole affair seriously enough, Monsieur le Deputé. Monsieur Levasin doesn't have the slightest intention of taking a shot at you, any more than you, I hope, have any intention of taking a shot at him. It's just a matter of keeping up appearances. You'll each have one shot in the air, and that's all!

MANNEQUIN-LEADER: But how do you know what designs Monsieur Levasin may have on me? Once for no reason at all he punched me in the head; why wouldn't he now take a shot at me, particularly if it gives him pleasure?

GENTLEMAN 1: Monsieur le Deputé likes to joke. (*Laughs*) Hee-hee-hee! That's a good one – for no reason at all! After all, he did find his wife in your arms, and what's more she was pretty completely undressed. We all know, *entre nous*, that Madame Levasin has never been distinguished by the strictness of her morals. It would have been one thing if he'd found you together without witnesses. You may rest assured that, as a cultured gentleman, he wouldn't have started any row over such a trifle. It was quite another thing to find you in the presence of so many witnesses. He had no other choice but to react exactly as he did. Monsieur Levasin asked us to take this occasion to express to you his profound regret on account of this entire unpleasant incident. Monsieur Levasin would like, for the sake of your common interests, to bring this unpleasant affair to a conclusion as soon as possible. That is why the duel must be arranged immediately. After the duel you will shake hands, and the whole thing will be settled. Really, there is no reason for you to feel unfriendly toward him. It would be more understandable for you to have such feelings toward Monsieur Arnaux who after all publicly ordered you out of his house. Such an insult cannot be washed away even by a pistol shot.

GENTLEMAN 2: So you'll allow us to convey your challenge to Monsieur Levasin. The choice of weapons and all other details kindly leave to us. Pistols with an unrifled barrel, at twenty-five paces – pure

Dmitri Moor: Illustrations for Bruno Jasieński's *Mannequins' Ball*.
7. Act III, Scene 4. The duel between the Mannequin-Leader and manufacturer Levasin is arranged among the seconds.

formalities. At such a distance a bullet even if it hits its mark will at worst only perforate the suit one's wearing.

MANNEQUIN-LEADER: A fine business! I'm not at all anxious to come back to the atelier, that is, I meant to say, to come home, in a perforated frock-coat.

GENTLEMAN 1: Monsieur le Deputé is still in a jocular mood. I guess you've already made your arrangements. You must have authorized somebody else to represent you. Is that right?

MANNEQUIN-LEADER: Take it as you will.

GENTLEMAN 1: So I guessed right. Allow us then to apologize to you for our persistence and to hasten to reassure Monsieur Levasin that you are not in the least angry with him.

MANNEQUIN-LEADER: I am not in the least angry. You may tell him that.

(GENTLEMEN 1 and 2 *bow and withdraw to the ballroom.*)

SCENE 5

(*Almost at the same time* GENTLEMEN 3 *and* 4 *appear at the left door. Both head toward the* LEADER.)

GENTLEMAN 3: Monsieur le Deputé Ribandel? I'm afraid we have been anticipated. We should like to offer you our services if this privilege has not already been granted to somebody else.

MANNEQUIN-LEADER: And what services do you offer?

GENTLEMAN 4: We should like to offer you our services as seconds in the upcoming duel.

MANNEQUIN-LEADER: And where did you get that idea?

GENTLEMAN 4: We've come partly at the request of Monsieur Arnaux. Monsieur Arnaux, as you may well imagine, is very grieved by the sudden turn affairs have taken. His only hope is that you'll understand that in the presence of so many witnesses he could not have acted otherwise. Do not think for a moment his order that you leave his house was meant seriously. Monsieur Arnaux would be happy to see this regrettable affair settled as soon as possible. An immediate duel will settle the question.

MANNEQUIN-LEADER: Whaaat? Does Monsieur Arnaux want to take a shot at me too?

GENTLEMAN 3: Not in the least. The thing is for you to fight a duel with Monsieur Levasin. By removing the insult and satisfying generally accepted social customs, you'll enable Monsieur Arnaux to take his words back. Believe me, this state of affairs is no less distressing to Monsieur Arnaux than to you.

MANNEQUIN-LEADER: What's all this talk about something distressing someone? Monsieur Arnaux demanded that I leave his house? With the greatest of pleasure! All I want is for them to open the door and let me out of here. I'll go immediately.

GENTLEMAN 3: Monsieur Arnaux will be extremely grieved and upset if we repeat your words to him. They seem to intimate that you still feel offended with him, and that you refuse to take into consideration the peculiar predicament in which he found himself. Really, you're not being just to Monsieur Arnaux. It's understandable if you feel resentment toward Monsieur Levasin. The insult done you by him cannot be washed away even by a pistol shot.

GENTLEMAN 4: This is the most opportune moment, the guests are tired, and many of them have gone to sleep in the far-off rooms. We'll find pistols and swords in Monsieur Arnaux's study. As to the place? (*Looks around the room.*) Well, this room is as good as any. (*Measures the stage by paces.*) A little over twenty-five paces. Among the guests, there are three physicians, and one of them is a surgeon. As though it had been planned in advance.

MANNEQUIN-LEADER: And what do we need physicians for? Has somebody been taken ill?

GENTLEMAN 4: Well, surely there can't be a duel without a physician. I'd refuse to be a second if there were no doctor. Any little scratch or wound requires medical assistance on the spot. As a matter of principle I won't go to a duel unless there's an experienced doctor on hand.

MANNEQUIN-LEADER: Aha. It's a very good principle.

GENTLEMAN 4: You may wholly rely on me in this affair. Can you handle a sword?

MANNEQUIN-LEADER: Handle a what?

GENTLEMAN 4: A sword. No? In that case it's best to use firearms. Unrifled barrels, twenty-five paces, child's play. Leave it to us. You just sit down and rest after a sleepless night. Right here, in this armchair would be best. I'll have a footman bring you a glass of champagne to refresh you. (*Forces the* MANNEQUIN-LEADER *into the armchair.*) Please don't distress yourself any more. It will be over in no time at all.

(GENTLEMEN 3 *and* 4 *rapidly withdraw to the right door.*)

GENTLEMAN 4: (*From the door*) We'll be back with the pistols in five minutes.

MANNEQUIN-LEADER: (*Jumps up*) Just what do you mean with the pistols? I beg your pardon! Wait a minute!

(GENTLEMEN 3 *and* 4 *have already left.*)

MANNEQUIN-LEADER: (*Enraged, bangs his fist down on the table and, inadvertently, presses the electric bell.*) Not on your life!

SCENE 6

LACKEY 1: (*Appears at the door to the right.*) Monsieur le Deputé, did you ring?

MANNEQUIN-LEADER: (*In confusion*) Yes, it seems I did ... inadvertently ... I rested my arm on it.

LACKEY 2: That's no cause for concern! (*Pause*) Monsieur le Deputé, may we move the furniture?

(*Enter* LACKEY 2. *The two* LACKEYS *begin to move furniture back to the wall, clearing the center of the stage.*)

MANNEQUIN-LEADER: What actually are you doing?

LACKEY 1: Monsieur de la Grange has ordered us to move the furniture to the wall and clear the center of the salon for a distance of twenty-five paces.

MANNEQUIN-LEADER: Twenty-five paces? When did he manage to tell you that?

LACKEY 1: Just now. He was running upstairs and on his way he gave the order: "Clear the foyer," he said, "take the furniture away, don't let any of the guests into the adjoining rooms. Stand guard at the door. I'll run up for the pistols."

MANNEQUIN-LEADER: (*To* LACKEY 1.) Listen, my dear fellow. Before Monsieur de la Grange returns, I must run out for a minute to attend to some business. Open the door for me.

LACKEY 1: It can't be done, Monsieur le Deputé. Even if we let Monsieur le Deputé out, the police would detain you anyhow. The order is not to let anyone out under any pretext whatsoever.

MANNEQUIN-LEADER: (*Fidgets, clearly nervous. After a short pause.*) Tell me, is there often shooting here?

LACKEY 1: (*Amazed*) Shooting?

MANNEQUIN-LEADER: Well, yes! Taking shots at one another or fighting with swords?

LACKEY 2: (*Astonished*) With swords?

LACKEY 1: Monsieur le Deputé wants to ask whether any duels ever take place here?

MANNEQUIN-LEADER: Yes, that's it. Is it something that necessarily happens at every ball?

LACKEY 1: Oh, no, of course not! Here at Monsieur Arnaux's it never happens. This is an exceptional case. But at my former master's, at Count d'Armenanville's, a month didn't pass by there without someone shooting somebody else. Now it was over women, then over horses, now over this, now over that. Once it was even over dogs: as to which one jumped better. Once some Spaniard shot off two of the Count's son's fingers.

MANNEQUIN-LEADER: (*Glances nervously at his hand.*) His fingers?

LACKEY 1: And whenever the young masters went out into the forest at dawn to fight with swords, they would often come back minus something or other. Some marquis once lopped off the young Count de la Tour's hand. They stitched it back on several times, but it wouldn't grow together.

MANNEQUIN-LEADER: Lopped off his hand? Entirely? (*Nervously feels his left hand and makes a few gymnastic exercises with his hand.*)

LACKEY 1: Slashed right through.

MANNEQUIN-LEADER: And have you ever been involved in that kind of a shooting match?

LACKEY 1: Me? (*Laughs*) Monsieur le Deputé likes to make jokes! We are simple folk. We settle such matters in a simple fashion. Somebody smacks you in the jaw, and you wallop him back straight in the mug so that he sees stars. And that's the end of it.

MANNEQUIN-LEADER: My dear fellows, I have very urgent business, I'll return immediately. Please open the door. I'll work it out somehow with the police.

ANGÉLIQUE: (*Enters by the left door; to the* LACKEYS.) You may go.

(*The* LACKEYS *go out.*)

SCENE 7

ANGÉLIQUE: Monsieur Ribandel, listen to me. After everything that's happened, you probably didn't think that I'd want to talk to you. You'll be surprised if I tell you that I'm not angry with you! I know it's all her fault. Don't take daddy's words too seriously. In his place you would have acted in exactly the same way. Everything will come out all right. Now that you have sent your seconds to Levasin...

MANNEQUIN-LEADER: Me? But I have...

ANGÉLIQUE: Don't deny it. I know all about it. You have behaved as a gentleman should! The insult you suffered at Levasin's hands rules out the possibility of your having any dealings with him ever again. This will certainly make it easier to arrange your reconciliation with daddy. Your duel with Levasin opens the door for daddy to make peace with you.

MANNEQUIN-LEADER: Very glad to hear it. But first of all I would like someone to open the door for me, which nobody seems to be willing to do.

ANGÉLIQUE: The duel will open it for you.

MANNEQUIN-LEADER: Much obliged for your kindness, but then it may be too late.

ANGÉLIQUE: Why? Do a few hours mean so much to you?

(ARNAUX *appears at the door from the ballroom.* LEVASIN *appears simultaneously at the right door. Both of them fail to notice* ANGÉLIQUE *who is screened off by the back of an armchair. Both walk toward the* MANNEQUIN-LEADER.)

ARNAUX AND LEVASIN: (*Together*) Monsieur Ribandel! ...

(*They notice each other and cough nervously.* ARNAUX *notices his daughter.*)

ARNAUX: Angélique, leave us, my child!

ANGÉLIQUE: (*Rises and walks out. Passing her father, she mutters.*) What brought you here? Who asked for you? I would have had him totally under my thumb ...

(MANNEQUIN-LEADER, *whistling demonstratively, leaves by the left door.*)

SCENE 8

ARNAUX: (*By the window; after a short pause.*) It's going to be rainy today. The sky is overcast ...

LEVASIN: I wonder how long we'll be under siege. Funny story, isn't it?

ARNAUX: In any case, you wouldn't have been able to get back home. The police have kept all automobiles away from the entrance so they won't block the street and stir up the rabble.

LEVASIN: It seems to me the police have gone a little too far in their zealousness. It would have been possible to have cleaned up this whole mess without any uproar and without blowing it up to huge proportions. That a strike was expected in your plants was known even to the sparrows chirping in the trees ... But I doubt whether your mansion is really exposed to any danger.

ARNAUX: Of course. Particularly since there won't be any strike in my plants, no matter how much some people may want it ... By morning all this will be a thing of the past.

·LEVASIN: By morning? That sounds a bit too optimistic. Of course, if the management meets the demands of the workers, well, then, of course, it's possible.

ARNAUX: That's not the only way. There are others. For instance, the workers may drop their demands.

LEVASIN: Of course, such things are possible, but of late they have been happening rather rarely. True, they say, miracles happen, but that's a matter of faith.

ARNAUX: "Miracles" occur where there's nothing supernatural. (*Telephone rings.* ARNAUX *takes the receiver.*) Yes! … What? … Have you gone mad! What proclamation? … Who signed it? … When was that? … How much? … Have you lost your mind? … That can't be! … What? … Hello! … Hello! … Damn it! (*Bangs the receiver rest up and down furiously.*) Hello! … (*Slams down the receiver.*) Disconnected …

LEVASIN: (*Venomously*) Well, how about it now? Do you still believe in miracles?

ARNAUX: That's incredible. Where is that man?

LEVASIN: (*Through his teeth.*) In our present economic situation faith in miracles, even non-supernatural miracles, is, as you yourself can see, something quite illusory. You'll recall that I warned you against such a cutthroat game and proposed that we do that business together. In your calculations you forgot one simple truth – proverbs are the wisdom of the people and there's an old saying that "He laughs best who laughs last."

(*Telephone rings.*)

ARNAUX: (*Hastily grabs the receiver.*) Hello! … Who? … Levasin? (*Hands* LEVASIN *the receiver.*) For you.

LEVASIN: (*Takes the receiver from* ARNAUX.) It's me … Yes! … Who is speaking? … What? … Have you gone mad? … Which proclamation? Ribandel signed it? When was that? … A five franc increase? … Have you gone crazy! … It's been announced? You're delirious! … At what time? … At three? … I spoke to him personally at half past two … Well, yes! … He gave me absolutely foolproof guarantees … What's to be done now? … How in hell do I know what to do? … No, he hasn't left. He's here … Call ten minutes from now. I'll clear it up right away. (*Slams down the receiver.*) It's incredible! Where is that man?

ARNAUX: He was here a minute ago.

LEVASIN: He went out through that door.

(*Both of them dash to the left door; in the doorway they knock against the* MANNEQUIN-LEADER.)

SCENE 9

MANNEQUIN-LEADER: (*Politely stepping aside.*) I beg your pardon!

ARNAUX: (*Seizes him by the shoulder.*) Monsieur Ribandel! There's been some kind of misunderstanding. I've just received a call from my plant. Your union has gone out on strike, after having made demands twice as great as those of the Communists. They maintain that the order was signed by you. They say that long before all that happened here today, delegates from the union came to you for instructions at three in the morning. Is that true?

LEVASIN: (*Tears the* MANNEQUIN-LEADER *out of* ARNAUX's *hands and shakes him.*) Monsieur Ribandel, there's been some kind of mis-understanding. I've just received a call that your union has declared a strike in my plant. They demand an increase. They maintain that all this has taken place according to your orders. Is that true?

MANNEQUIN-LEADER: (*Freeing himself from his hands.*) Excuse me, gentlemen, but you better keep your hands to yourselves. Only a moment ago you didn't want to speak to me.

ARNAUX: Monsieur Ribandel, this is no time for nonsense. Tell me that it's all untrue.

LEVASIN: Tell me that it's not so!

MANNEQUIN-LEADER: (*Retreats before the advancing* ARNAUX *and* LEVASIN.) Gentlemen, I beg you, please keep your hands to your-selves. The second time around this has ceased to be funny. If you hit me in the head one more time, I'll sock you so hard that you'll see streams of shooting stars before your eyes!

ARNAUX: (*Roaring*) So it was true?

LEVASIN: It was true? Speak up immediately!

MANNEQUIN-LEADER: Did I ever tell you anything untrue? Of course it's the truth.

ARNAUX: Whaaat? And what about the money you took from me?

LEVASIN: And from me …

ARNAUX: Give the money back!

LEVASIN: Return the money to me immediately.

MANNEQUIN-LEADER: Hold on. I can't return the money, I gave it away.

ARNAUX: Gave it to who?

LEVASIN: That's a swindle pure and simple!

MANNEQUIN-LEADER: I beg your pardon! I gave it away to be used for the same purpose you had given it to me for. I gave it to the strike committee.

ARNAUX AND LEVASIN: (*Together*) Whaaat?

Dmitri Moor: Illustrations for Bruno Jasieński's *Mannequins' Ball.*
8. Act III, Scene 8. The seconds measure the duelling ground.

MANNEQUIN-LEADER: (*To* LEVASIN) Didn't you yourself say you were contributing the money to the strike fund?

LEVASIN: Don't play the fool!

MANNEQUIN-LEADER: (*To* ARNAUX) And didn't you give me the money as a contribution to the fund for the first rational strike in your plants?

ARNAUX: Embezzler!

LEVASIN: Fraud!

ARNAUX AND LEVASIN: (*Together*) Swine!

(*Enter six Gentlemen: four seconds, a referee and a physician. The* SECONDS *carry a case of pistols.*)

SCENE 10

The SECONDS *hasten to separate the quarreling gentlemen.*

GENTLEMAN 5: Gentlemen!

GENTLEMAN 3: Gentlemen!

GENTLEMAN 4: It's unheard of for the adversaries to converse together and even abuse one another before the duel itself!

GENTLEMAN 5: Calm down, calm down! Get control of yourselves, gentlemen!

(GENTLEMAN 6 *hurries in with two glasses of water. Hands one to* LEVASIN *and one to the* MANNEQUIN-LEADER.)

MANNEQUIN-LEADER: Thank you. (*Takes the glass.*)

LEVASIN: (*Rudely pushes the* GENTLEMAN 6 *with the glass aside.*) Leave me alone! Enough of this comedy!

GENTLEMAN 5: Monsieur Levasin, you are insulting the seconds. I thought that you would show greater self-control before the duel.

LEVASIN: (*In a rage*) Give me that stinking gun, I'll shoot him down like a dog!

GENTLEMAN 5: Monsieur Levasin, all exclamations and threats on the duelling terrain are a sign of bad manners. I call you to order. (*To all present.*) Gentlemen, be so kind as to take your places. I am measuring the terrain. (*Measures the stage by paces*) One, two, three … (*to himself*) twenty-four, twenty-five. Now take your places, if you please.

MANNEQUIN-LEADER: But I … I am not at all …

GENTLEMEN 3 *and* 4 *forcibly put him in his place.*

GENTLEMAN 3: Here is your place, Monsieur le Deputé.

GENTLEMAN 4: (*Puts a pistol in his hand.*) The trigger is cocked, please, don't pull it.

GENTLEMAN 3: We'll count three. Yours is the first shot!

GENTLEMAN 4: Raise your pistol straight up, please. That's it. At the word "three," you lower your pistol and shoot. Then you lower your pistol muzzle down and stand motionless until your opponent shoots.

MANNEQUIN-LEADER: Stand until he shoots?

GENTLEMAN 4: Yes. Absolutely motionless. It'll be for just a minute. (*Adjusts the lapels of the* MANNEQUIN-LEADER's *frock coat.*) Now, at the given signal, you shoot first.

MANNEQUIN-LEADER: Yes, but I don't even know how to shoot!

GENTLEMAN 4: That doesn't matter, you don't need to know how. You just squeeze the trigger with your index finger. (*Grabs his hand.*) Not now, for god's sake! When you hear "three."

MANNEQUIN-LEADER: And does he know how to shoot?

GENTLEMAN 4: Most likely he doesn't know either. Besides, I've told you already it doesn't really matter. Those who don't know how to shoot usually hit the mark better than those who do.

MANNEQUIN-LEADER: A nice prospect!

GENTLEMAN 5: Attention!

MANNEQUIN-LEADER: If he hit me in the head, it wouldn't be half-bad.

GENTLEMAN 4: Just the opposite! What are you saying? In the head – God forbid!

MANNEQUIN-LEADER: Oh, if I knew for sure it would be in the head, it would be a breeze.

GENTLEMAN 5: Ready! I am beginning to count. At the word "three," Monsieur Ribandel shoots.

GENTLEMAN 4: (*In a whisper.*) Attention! I'll give you the signal.

GENTLEMAN 5: (*Counts*) One … two … three. (*Silence*)

GENTLEMAN 4: (*Whispers in despair*) Go ahead and shoot!

MANNEQUIN-LEADER: (*Shoots; pause*) Well, of course I haven't hit him. I knew it in advance. And he'll hit me for sure. If only it's in the head!

GENTLEMAN 4: (*Reproachfully*) Monsieur le Deputé, why such gloomy thoughts? Lower your hand with the pistol. That's it. Now you must stand perfectly motionless for one minute.

GENTLEMAN 5: Ready? I am beginning to count. At the word "three," Monsieur Levasin shoots. Attention! I ask you not to change your position under any circumstances. One …

(*Suddenly the lights go out. Darkness.*)

VOICES IN THE DARK: Lights! What's the matter?

VOICE OF THE LACKEY: Gentlemen, don't get excited. There's been a power failure.

VOICE OF GENTLEMAN 3: Bring candles!

VOICE OF GENTLEMAN 2: This looks like a general strike!

VOICE OF LEVASIN: Those Communist scoundrels evidently have not been sleeping.

VOICE OF GENTLEMAN 4: Bring some light over here!

VOICE OF THE LACKEY: Just a moment, gentlemen.

(*Enter* LACKEYS *carrying candelabra. In the light it becomes evident that the* MANNEQUIN-LEADER *has opened the window and is making ready to leap out.* GENTLEMAN 1 *seizes him by the tail of his coat.*)

GENTLEMAN 1: Monsieur le Deputé, where are you going?

MANNEQUIN-LEADER: Me? I was just going for a minute, to get matches.

GENTLEMAN 1: We have candles here. There's quite enough light. We may proceed.

MANNEQUIN-LEADER: I am afraid he won't see well enough.

GENTLEMAN 3: Don't worry. There's enough light, he'll see all right.

(*The* LACKEYS *bring in more candelabra.*)

MANNEQUIN-LEADER: Maybe we should postpone it after all?

LEVASIN: Oh, the son of a bitch! First he stirs up trouble, and now it's too dark for him! No, my dear fellow, you won't get out of here alive!

GENTLEMAN 5: Monsieur Levasin. I warned you that on the duelling terrain all kinds of threats are out of place. This is the first time in my life that I have ever taken part in such a duel. Gentlemen, I ask you to take up your previous positions. I am beginning to count. At the word "three," Monsieur Levasin shoots. One …

(*This minute the window is crashed open, and a headless man leaps into the room – this is the real* LEADER Paul RIBANDEL.)

GENTLEMAN 5: Two …

LEADER: Stop (*General confusion*) Gentlemen, don't believe him! It's a hoax! I am Deputy Paul Ribandel. The one pretending to be me is not a human, but a mannequin. Those crooks stole my head. I am Deputy Paul Ribandel!

LACKEYS: (*Appearing at the right door*) Gentlemen, don't pay any attention to him. He's drunk. He's apparently coming back from a masquerade. (*They approach the* LEADER *and attempt to get hold of him.*)

MANNEQUIN-LEADER: (*Raises his hand*) Just a minute please. This gentleman is right! (*To the* LEADER) Dear Leader! You're just in time! I almost didn't recognize you. (*Shoves the pistol into his hands and pushes him into his own place.*) Please, here's your place. (*With a rapid gesture he removes his head like a hat.*) Please, here's your head! (*Hands the head over to the* LEADER.) Take it. Take it quickly! I've had enough of it! I was tempted for nothing! When I won the head, I was happy. I thought I'd found a treasure. To hell with your head! Now I know what you need it for! We made the right decision to cut off that bad apple's head. (*Points to the* LEADER.) But what's the use? Can we cut off all your heads? There aren't enough scissors. And it's really not our business. Others are coming who can do a better job than we could. We thought you were only torturing us. It seems there are others ready to settle old scores with you. Looks as if they really mean business now. You won't have to wait long! But in the meantime, since they all have their heads, why should you be different? Take it. (*Places the head on the* LEADER's *shoulders. Slaps it down with the palm of his hand so that it fits better. Then straightens the* LEADER's *necktie and adjusts the lapels of his frock coat. To all present.*) Gentlemen, you may proceed. Leader, you have had your shot. I ask you to stand absolutely motionless. Monsieur the referee! (*Waves his hand*) Three. Monsieur Levasin's shot. (*Leaps through the window.*)

Curtain

THE END